the broken world of tennessee williams

madison and milwaukee 1965

the university of wisconsin press

the broken world of tennessee williams

esther merle jackson

Published by
The University of Wisconsin Press
Madison and Milwaukee
P.O. Box 1379
Madison, Wisconsin 53701

Printed in the United States of America by
Vail-Ballou Press, Inc., Binghamton, New York

Library of Congress Catalog Card Number 64-8489

to my father

preface

When Tennessee Williams' poetic drama *The Glass Menagerie* opened in New York in 1945, a new epoch in the history of Western theatre began. For with this play Williams seemed to succeed Eugene O'Neill as the chief architect of form in the American drama. In the decade which followed, the American theatre was to produce at least one other major dramatist as well as a number of minor playwrights of merit. In 1964, some nineteen years later, it is a matter of general critical agreement that Williams remains one of the pivotal figures in the "American school." Although Tennessee Williams is a writer less highly regarded by many critics than Eugene O'Neill, Thornton Wilder, William Saroyan, or Arthur Miller, he has, nonetheless, exerted a decisive influence on the development of form in the contemporary theatre. His influence, especially in relation to the interpretation of character and dramatic action, may be seen in the work of Europeans such as John Osborne, Harold Pinter, and Jean Genêt, as well as in that of Americans such as William Inge, Paddy Chayefsky, and Edward Albee.

Williams' claim to the status of a major dramatist rests, in large measure, on the critical and popular acceptance accorded four works: *The Glass Menagerie* (1945), *A Streetcar Named Desire* (1947), *Summer and Smoke* (1948), and *Cat on a Hot Tin Roof* (1955). While some critics have found greater literary merit in the works of O'Neill, Wilder, Saroyan, Miller, and Clifford Odets, the fact remains that Williams, since the first decade of his Broadway activity, has been the most popular playwright in the life of the American theatre, and one of the most widely performed dramatists in the history of the Western stage.[1] Despite the critical controversy which has attended his career in the theatre, Williams has won a substantial measure of acceptance as a serious writer. One of the earliest signs of this recognition was the prize awarded the young artist in 1933 by the Writers' Guild of St. Louis, Missouri. In 1939 he was the recipient of an award given by the Group Theatre of New

1. Since 1945, Williams has had produced on Broadway twelve full-length works (see the Appendix). At this writing, nine of these plays have been made into films. The film *Baby Doll* (1956) was composed from two short plays from the collection *American Blues.*

Theodore Shank reports in *The Educational Theatre Journal* (XIII [May, 1961], 113) that *The Glass Menagerie* was the play most frequently produced by American college and university groups between 1955 and 1960. *The Glass Menagerie,* over this four-year period, had one hundred and three productions, as compared with ninety-three for Miller's play *The Crucible,* seventy-three for Wilder's *Our Town,* and fifty-five for *The Taming of the Shrew.* A report on 1961–62 in *The Educational Theatre Journal* (XV [May, 1963], 165) lists Williams as the most frequently produced modern playwright in American college and university theatre.

The author's agent, Miss Audrey Wood (of the Ashley Famous Artists Agency, Inc.), reports that permissions have been granted for productions of *The Glass Menagerie* in thirty-six countries outside of the United States of America; for *A Streetcar Named Desire* in thirty-six countries; and for *Cat on a Hot Tin Roof* in twenty-eight (see the Appendix).

York. In 1940 he won the coveted Rockefeller Fellowship for playwriting. In 1944 he was cited for his achievement by the National Institute of Arts and Letters. The work of his mature years has, thus far, won the playwright three Critics' Circle Awards (1945, 1947, and 1955), two Pulitzer Prizes (1947 and 1955), and membership in the National Institute of Arts and Letters (1952).

The emergence of Tennessee Williams as a major dramatist is a significant development in American cultural history. Study of the details of his career points up significant parallels. In an important sense, the theatre of Tennessee Williams is an aspect of a second American Renaissance, which, like the first, followed a great war. In the same way as the theatre of Eugene O'Neill seemed to emerge out of the heightened national consciousness which marked the close of World War I, so the theatre of Tennessee Williams seems to have been an expression of a new sense of identity which American arts and letters reflected at the conclusion of World War II. Certainly by 1945, the political, social, and intellectual climate of America had become more favorable to the idea of a distinctively American drama than it had been at any time before. Moreover, by mid-century the theatre had succeeded in establishing many of the conditions necessary for popular acceptance of an American dramatic kind. Out of the experimentation of O'Neill, Wilder, Saroyan, Odets, Elmer Rice, John Howard Lawson, and Paul Green there had emerged a rich and complex American theatrical convention, possessing its own catalogue of themes, characters, modes of speech, styles of acting, and patterns of visual design. This conventionalized theatrical language had found a vital complement in an emerging art of the *mise en scène,* in a distinctively American system of directing and design which had been given strong impetus in the work of Arthur Hopkins, Robert Edmond Jones, Cleon Throckmorton, Norman Bel Geddes, Mordecai Gorelik, and Lee Simonson.[2]

2. The stage director Arthur Hopkins (1878–1950) is important for his

Other conditions affecting Williams' marked success as a playwright had their origins in more comprehensive patterns of cultural growth. Like the popular dramatists of the Elizabethan age, he found a rich source of theatrical material in the patterns of common expression emerging in his native land. The success of *The Glass Menagerie* may be traced in part to his effective use of idiomatic forms, especially to his ability to mediate between the world of ideas and the language of the common man. As in the Elizabethan age, the talent for translating into a universal language the philosophical perceptions, political events, and social conditions of an age brought to the playwright and his theatre a large and varied audience.

Although *The Glass Menagerie* promised a new epoch in American stage history, it was not as revolutionary as it seemed. For the play shared a significant distribution of characteristics with such earlier works as *The Adding Machine* (1923), *Strange Interlude* (1928), *Awake and Sing* (1935), *Our Town* (1938), and *The Time of Your Life* (1939). Moreover, elements of its form could be traced to European antecedents, not only to the work of modern dramatists such as Strindberg, Chekhov, and Pirandello, but to the entire literature of revolt which had its formal beginning in that movement described as *Sturm und Drang*. Perhaps the most revolutionary characteristic of *The Glass Menagerie* was that in its total concept it reflected an imaginative quality—a vision of reality—which was clearly and unmistakably American.

The presence of this distinctive quality was not accidental. According to Williams, *The Glass Menagerie* had been designed specifically for the popular American audience. It was, in this sense, an especially significant achievement, for it opposed Williams to the theatre of purely traditional forms. It represented his public commitment to the creation of a popular art. With

service as a link between the experimental advances of Eugene O'Neill, Robert Edmond Jones, and Kenneth Macgowan and the commercial theatre of the twenties.

this play Williams fulfilled the mandate of Walt Whitman, uttered almost a century before. He succeeded in the evocation of a living form, created from the emergent American consciousness.

The opening of *The Glass Menagerie* in 1945, like the production of *Le Cid* in 1636 [3] or the performance of *Le Docteur amoureux* in 1658 or the revival of *The Seagull* in 1898, marked the beginning of a new epoch in Western theatre history. Apparently Williams was conscious of his role in an historic development. In the manifesto that prefaced the published edition of the play, he wrote "These remarks are not meant as a preface only to this particular play. They have to do with a conception of a new, plastic theatre which must take the place of the exhausted theatre of realistic conventions if the theatre is to resume vitality as a part of our culture." [4] For Williams, "vitality" was associated with the return of the theatre to its natural functions: to joyous and irreverent entertainment, to shock and terror, to symbol-making, and to the figurative exploration of life. He proposed to recover these purposes by re-establishing the creative relationship of the drama to idiomatic forms of expression. Like Shakespeare, Corneille, Molière, and Lope, Williams effected his restoration by introducing into traditional structures modes of expression drawn from all levels of experience. Many years before the appearance of *The Glass Menagerie* he had begun this process of adapting traditional forms to the vivid, vulgar, and energetic modes of expression which appeared in the cinema, the soap opera, and the radio jingle; at street corners, revival meetings, and political debates; in jazz songs, brass bands, and children's games. He wrote of this motive: "In this scene I am trying to catch the quality of really 'tough' Americana of the comic sheets, the skid-row bars, cathouses, Grade B movies, street-Arabs, vagrants, drunks, pitchmen, gamblers, whores, all the rootless, unstable and highly

3. Recent scholarship suggests that *Le Cid* may have opened in 1637.

4. Tennessee Williams, Production Notes for *The Glass Menagerie*, p. ix. (For full citations of Tennessee Williams' works, see the Appendix.)

spirited life beneath the middle-class social level in the States." [5]

This essentially poetic motive—that of seeking to interpret obscure realities in a universal language—had been seen in the work of other American dramatists, particularly in that of Thornton Wilder, Clifford Odets, and William Saroyan. But Williams, perhaps, had more comprehensive motives than those which had been apparent in plays such as *The Time of Your Life, Awake and Sing,* or *Our Town.* Like O'Neill, he conceived for popular theatre an ancient purpose: the exposure of human suffering. To this end, he had by 1945 developed extensive skills.

It has been characteristic of much American criticism that Williams' technical achievement has been seriously underestimated. Close students of his form find, however, that he conceals beneath the sensuous texture of his work a significant ability as a builder of play structure, a major skill as a narrator, and a high level of accomplishment as a writer of play dialogue and action. These abilities may be traced, in part, to the playwright's extended technical training and wide professional experiences. Throughout much of his career, Williams has worked in non-dramatic media as well as in theatre. Some of his early short stories have been published in the collections *One Arm and Other Stories* (1948) and *Hard Candy* (1954). His novel, *The Roman Spring of Mrs. Stone,* was published in 1950. Of direct influence on his idea of dramatic form has been his interest in poetry. Examples of his facility in this medium may be seen in the volume *In the Winter of Cities* (1956) and in the New Directions series XI, XII, XIII, and XIV.

While his technical skills have been of obvious value in the playwright's search for a representative form, his most important asset may be something less tangible, an acute "sense of theatre." Williams' clear interest in theatre for performance rather than in closet drama has involved him in constant con-

5. Tennessee Williams, *Ten Blocks on the Camino Real,* in *American Blues,* Block VII, p. 58.

troversy, particularly with critics of traditional schools. In the main, his subordination of literary interests to theatricality—playability—has left him less esteemed among academicians than Wilder or Miller; however, it has won for him the enthusiastic support of the theatre itself: of actors, directors, and scenic artists, who have maintained consistently high standards of interpretation for his plays. It has been this theatricality which has given to his drama that broad base of appeal which is vital to a popular art. In the sixties, the theatre of Williams is still finding new audiences through the successful transposition of his plays to allied arts—to radio, television, cinema, ballet, and modern dance.

In 1945 Williams was not in actuality a beginning playwright. He had spent a long and arduous apprenticeship in the theatre. Like Molière, he learned the rudiments of his craft away from the restrictive influence of commercial theatre. Despite his predilection for popular forms, Williams may be described, in one sense, as a "university dramatist." Like O'Neill, Miller, Paul Green, and others in the American school, he acquired much of his knowledge of the traditional theatre—its theories, literature, and practice—in an academic setting. His illuminating essays and well-formed critical theories testify to his studies at St. Louis' Washington University, the State University of Iowa, and New York's New School for Social Research. Perhaps more important than the formal knowledge he gained from these studies was that aesthetic and philosophical orientation which the American universities of the twenties, thirties, and forties gave to young artists. Like the Elizabethan universities, the French Academy of the seventeenth century, and the vigorous German universities in the time of Goethe, the American universities of the twentieth century have provided artistic apprentices, such as Williams was in the thirties, with a system of linguistic conventions; that is, with a syntax common to the entire fabric of the developing arts.

But if Williams acquired that theoretical background necessary to develop his idea of form in the university, he gained a technical understanding of drama in the theatre itself. Again like Molière, he put together his vigorous and irreverent style of writing under the influence of a young and talented provincial company. In the Introduction to *27 Wagons Full of Cotton,* he has written of his period of apprenticeship with "The Mummers" of St. Louis, Missouri:

> The Mummers of St. Louis were my professional youth. They were the disorderly theater group of St. Louis, standing socially, if not also artistically, opposite to the usual Little Theater group. . . .
>
> Dynamism was what The Mummers had, and for about five years—roughly from about 1935 to 1940—they burned like one of Miss Millay's improvident little candles—and then expired. Yes, there was about them that kind of excessive romanticism which is youth and which is the best and purest part of life.
>
> . . . .
>
> They put on bad shows sometimes, but they never put on a show that didn't deliver a punch to the solar plexus, maybe not in the first act, maybe not in the second, but always at last a good hard punch was delivered, and it made a difference in the lives of the spectators that they had come to that place and seen that show.[6]

It was during the thirties that Williams began to experiment seriously with his idea of dramatic form. The short plays of the series *27 Wagons Full of Cotton* and *American Blues* give some indication of the stage of development to which his work had come in the late thirties. Essentially, these plays seem to represent early experimentation with the same idea of form which was to result in the creation of *The Glass Menagerie.* They are immature expressions of a "plastic theatre," early examples of the kind of drama which the playwright would develop in the subsequent stages of his career.

Early in his professional career, Williams entered an association which was to assist him materially in the refinement of his production form. He became allied with a group of artists who for many years had been concerned with the development of an

6. Tennessee Williams, "Something Wild . . . ," in the Introduction to *27 Wagons Full of Cotton,* pp. viii–xii.

American art of the *mise en scène*. In the circle which included the director Elia Kazan, the designer Jo Mielziner, and the teacher and theorist Lee Strasberg, he found many of the conditions described by Gordon Craig as ideal. Out of this creative association emerged an appropriate dramaturgy for his theatre: an art of directing, acting, production, and design congruent with the demands of his texts. So effective has been this interpretative instrument created by Kazan and his artistic collaborators that its design for production has become conventionalized, not only as a pattern for the theatre of Williams but for the articulation of the work of other dramatists in the American school. Since 1945, this "American formalism" has taken its place in world theatre as a characteristic art of the *mise en scène.*

In the years since 1945 Tennessee Williams has continued to work toward the realization of his idea of form. The plays written since that time seem to repeat the pattern of organization introduced in the works of the first decade. Only *Period of Adjustment* (1960) seems to have varied definitively from the form introduced in *The Glass Menagerie.* An ironic comedy, *Period of Adjustment* seems a rather pleasant interlude that brightens the somber pattern of the playwright's more serious work.

Like Picasso, Williams seems to restate his creative experiences, to subject his poetic vision to continual reconsideration. He thus seems to reject the empirical approach to subject matter favored by the realists and appears, rather, to bring to a single subject progressive attitudes. A pattern of thematic recapitulation, visible as early as *The Glass Menagerie,* grows more pronounced in his later periods, when ideas, characters, plots, and portions of dialogue reappear with regularity. Accordingly, the chronology of his work is problematic. *You Touched Me* (1946), written in collaboration with Donald Windham, is one of Williams' early works. It was staged in 1943 at the Cleveland Playhouse by the director of the Dallas Theatre, Margo Jones. *Orpheus Descending* (1958) is a revision of a play, *Battle of Angels,* which closed during its Boston tryouts in 1940 and which was later retitled, for the cinema, *The Fugitive Kind,* after an even earlier work. *The Garden District* (1958) expanded a sketch called *Something Unspoken* from *27 Wagons Full of Cotton* (1946). *Sweet Bird of Youth* (1959) recalls to memory aspects of *A Streetcar Named Desire* (1947) and *Cat on a Hot Tin Roof* (1955). A recent success—as of this writing—was adapted from an early work of fiction: *The Night of the Iguana* (1962) is a reworking of a short story which appeared in the collection *One Arm and Other Stories* (1948).

Williams' idea of form is not then fully revealed in any single work. Like Henri Bergson, the playwright holds that the artist's view of reality is but the mirror of change. Williams suggests that each of his plays represents a glimpse of reality, a momentary image drawn out of the flux. He writes of his continuing effort to record his changing vision, "A play is never old until you stop working on it." [7]

This book represents an attempt to examine some aspects of the drama of Tennessee Williams. It is an attempt to describe the major characteristics of his developing form, especially to identify the powerful but changing idea of theatre which is reflected throughout the pattern of his work. While I do not wish to offer conclusive generalizations about the ultimate value of this playwright's achievements, I hope that it is possible to offer some observations which may facilitate the interpretation of this aspect of contemporary theatre history.

The plays themselves have provided the principal material for this study. I have sought to verify my observations with the evidence of Williams' critical essays and with the insights of related writings. It is my position that the achievement of Williams is based on the relevance of his drama to the major concerns of our time, and that his marked success as a popular dramatist may be traced to his ability to translate profound meanings into simple and effective theatrical language. It follows that his use of theme, character, myth, language, and scene

7. Tennessee Williams, "The Past, the Present and Perhaps," in the Introduction to *Orpheus Descending,* pp. ix–x.

is not accidental but is the result of a specific purpose: the creation of a new and relevant mode of contemporary dramatic expression.[8]

ESTHER M. JACKSON

Atlanta, Georgia
January 1964

8. Since this manuscript was completed, Williams has published his twelfth long work for the professional theatre. *The Milk Train Doesn't Stop Here Anymore* (1964) is a treatment of a short story published in 1959 by *Mademoiselle*. It is not a part of the material analyzed in this study.

acknowledgments

I am grateful to the editors of the following magazines for permission to reprint some of the material which has appeared, in somewhat different form, in earlier publications: "The Problem of Form in the Drama of Tennessee Williams," *College Language Association Journal* (Vol. IV, No. 1, September, 1960); "The Emergence of the Anti-hero in the Contemporary Drama," *The Central States Speech Journal* (Vol. XII, No. 2, February, 1961); and "Music and Dance as Elements of Form in the Drama of Tennessee Williams," *Revue d'Histoire du Théâtre* (*Actes du III° Congrès d'Histoire du Théâtre,* XV, No. 3, 1963).

As in all like circumstances, I am indebted to the generosity of many persons who have, in one way or another, contributed to this manuscript. I am deeply grateful to Mr. Williams, to his publishers, New Directions, and to his agent, Miss Audrey Wood, for graciously allowing me to quote extensively from his published works. I appreciate also having had an opportunity to talk with Mr. Williams' long-time director, Elia Kazan.

I should like to acknowledge a special debt of gratitude to my thesis committee at The Ohio State University, especially to my adviser, Professor Everett M. Schreck, for their help with my thesis, "The Emergence of a Characteristic Contemporary Form in the American Drama of Tennessee Williams." I wish also to express to Professors John H. Wilson, George R. Havens, Morris Weitz, and Charles Carlut of the Graduate Faculty my thanks for their advice and encouragement during the period of my graduate studies. I wish also to express my warm appreciation to Mrs. Isobel Korbel of the University of Wisconsin Press for her advice and assistance. I wish, finally, to express my appreciation to Mrs. Mary-Ellen James and to Mrs. Elizabeth Brantley for their help in the process of preparing this manuscript for publication.

I have been fortunate in having fellowship assistance during much of the time in which I have been engaged in this study. My thesis research was made possible through the assistance of fellowships awarded by the John Hay Whitney Foundation (1956–57) and by the Graduate School of The Ohio State University (1957–58). In 1960–61 I was the recipient of a Fulbright Research Grant, awarded for study in English stage history. While this book is not the direct result of that year's work, many aspects of its final form may be attributed to the findings of that related study.

Permission to reprint excerpts from Mr. Williams' books has been granted by his publishers, New Directions, although they have not read this work.

Permission to quote from Elia Kazan's "Notebook for *A Streetcar Named Desire*," a document previously published by the Bobbs-Merrill Company in the Toby Cole–Helen Chinoy book, *Directing the Play,* has been granted by Mr. Kazan.

Permission to quote from Volumes IV, VI, IX, and XVI of the authorized English translation of the works of C. G. Jung has been granted by the Bollingen Foundation, New York.

The excerpt from *Coleridge's Shakespearean Criticism* is reprinted by permission of Professor Thomas Middleton Raysor and of E. P. Dutton and Company, New York, publishers of the revised Everyman's Library Edition, released in 1960.

Excerpts from *Aristotle's Theory of Poetry and Fine Art* are taken from the English translation by S. H. Butcher, 4th edition revised, Dover Publications, Inc., New York.

Permission to quote from Jean-Paul Sartre's essay, "Forgers of Myths," was granted by the editors of *Theatre Arts Magazine,* New York.

Permission to quote from Edith Hamilton's book, *The Greek Way,* has been granted by W. W. Norton and Company, Inc., New York.

The excerpt from Edward Storer's translation of Luigi Pirandello's *Naked Masks,* ed. Eric Bentley, is reprinted by permission of E. P. Dutton and Company, and Dutton Paperback Series, New York.

The lines from Hart Crane's *The Broken Tower* are taken from *The Collected Poems of Hart Crane* ($3.95), Liveright Publishing Corp., New York.

The quotation from the Foreword to *Miss Julie,* in *Six Plays of Strindberg,* translated by Elizabeth Sprigge, is reprinted by permission of A. P. Watt and Son, London.

The line from Richard Eberhart's poem, *Reality! Reality! What is It?* is taken from his *Undercliff: Poems 1946–1953* (1953) and is reprinted by permission of the Oxford University Press.

The excerpt from Mark Van Doren's preface to *Four Great Tragedies,* taken from the Pocket Books Edition, is reprinted by permission of Holt, Rinehart, and Winston, Inc., New York.

The quotation from *Greek Tragedy* by H. D. F. Kitto is reprinted by permission of Methuen and Company, Ltd., London, and Barnes & Noble, Inc., New York.

Permission to reprint the excerpt from Jean-Paul Sartre's *No Exit* has been granted by Alfred A. Knopf, Inc., New York.

The excerpt from the Bosanquet-Bryant translation of the work of Georg W. F. Hegel is reprinted by permission of Routledge and Kegan Paul, Ltd., London.

Permission to quote from translations of Aeschylus and Euripides in *The Complete Greek Drama,* eds. Whitney J. Oates and Eugene O'Neill, Jr., has been granted by Random House, Inc., New York (copyright 1938). Permission to quote from the E. P. Coleridge translation of *Orestes* (which appears in *The Complete Greek Drama*) has been granted by G. Bell and Sons, Ltd., London.

The excerpt from E. Martin Browne's essay on Tennessee Williams has been taken from the Penguin Edition of *Cat on a Hot Tin Roof* and is reproduced by permission of Martin Secker and Warburg, Ltd., London.

The quotations from the transcript of the Bochum Festival discussion of *Camino Real* are reprinted by the kind permission of S. Fischer Verlag, Frankfurt-am-Main. The English translation, unpublished, is that of Professor Gerald Gillespie of the University of Southern California.

The excerpt from the Cloudesley Brereton and Fred Rothwell translation of Henri Bergson's *Laughter* is reprinted by permission of The Macmillan Company, New York.

Permission to quote from the works of T. S. Eliot has been granted by Harcourt, Brace, and World, Inc., New York.

Permission to quote from R. M. Albérès' book, *La Révolte des écrivains d'aujourd'hui,* has been granted by Éditions Buchet/Chastel, Paris.

The translation from Immanuel Kant's *Critique of Judgement* is by J. H. Bernard. Permission to quote from this work has been granted by St. Martin's Press, New York, and by Macmillan and Company, Ltd., London.

Permission to quote from Horace's *The Art of Poetry* has been granted by Harvard University Press and the Loeb Classical Library.

I should also like to thank the following sources for permission to use the photographs shown in the four pages of illustrations, following page 84.

The photograph of Tennessee Williams on the Broadway set of *A Streetcar Named Desire,* which appeared in *Life* Magazine, December 15, 1947, p. 101, was used with the permission of *Life* Magazine.

The photograph by Eileen Darby of the Broadway production of *A Streetcar Named Desire,* which appeared in *Theatre Arts* Magazine, February, 1948, p. 35, was used with the permission of Graphic House, Inc.

The photograph by Alfredo Valente of the Broadway production of *Camino Real,* which appeared in *Theatre Arts* Magazine, June, 1953, p. 14, was used with the permission of Alfredo Valente.

The photographs of Burl Ives (Big Daddy in *Cat on a Hot Tin Roof*) and Geraldine Page and Paul Newman (Princess and Chance in *Sweet Bird of Youth*) were used with the permission of Graphic House, Inc.

contents

list of illustrations

the broken world
of tennessee williams

chapter one

"REALITY! REALITY! WHAT IS IT?"

What is the nature of form in the drama? A review of the history of Western theatre suggests that there have been at least four significant answers to this question. Certainly, to say that there have been only four definitions of dramatic form in Western theatre is to simplify history to accommodate discussion. Obviously there have been innumerable varieties of drama, and these in turn have been interpreted in countless theories of form. In the opinion of historians such as John Gassner,[1] however, only a few of these kinds—and their theories—have

NOTE TO CHAPTER TITLE: This quotation is from a poem of the same name by Richard Eberhart and is taken from his *Undercliff: Poems 1946–1953* (1953), pp. 20–21; it is reprinted by permission of Oxford University Press.

1. See John Gassner, *Masters of the Drama* (3d ed. rev.; New York, 1954).

attained that level of maturation which must be accounted significant. Gassner, like other twentieth-century aestheticians, offers a theory of drama that finds form and the definition of form subject to constant change.[2] He interprets classic, neoclassic, romantic, and realistic definitions as attempts to describe the nature of dramatic form; each of these theories, however, incorporates within itself the bias of its own age.

Despite critical divergences among them, all four of these concepts share a common attribute: each confirms Aristotle's definition of form as the imitation of reality.[3] Dramatic form, however, is not mere physical representation. It is an attempt to distill from experience that which is essential and to project this reality into the concrete shape of theatrical performance. Drama, like that reality which it signifies, is multiform; that is, it is a complex of representations, some of which are materialistic in character, others of which are ideal in nature. The dramatic form possesses that which may be described as a "substantial identity," an ideal nature in the world of eternal truth.[4] But it has, in addition, a material character as a sensible shape; that is, it exists as a complex of plot, character, thought, lyric, dialogue, and spectacle. Aristotle's brief comment on catharsis suggests yet a third identity, an ephemeral existence deriving from the momentary interaction of author, spectator, and performer. Form in the drama, then, is the imitation of reality, but of reality in all its complexity. It attempts to provide a living image of the fundamental structure of human experience. It

2. See, in this connection, Susanne Langer, *Problems of Art: Ten Philosophical Lectures* (New York, 1957). See also Erich Auerbach, *Mimesis: The Representation of Reality in Western Literature,* trans. Willard Trask (Princeton, 1953).

3. See S. H. Butcher, trans., *Aristotle's Theory of Poetry and Fine Art: With a Critical Text and Translation of* The Poetics (4th ed., rev., New York, 1951), p. 124.

4. Butcher notes (p. 114) that a clear understanding of Aristotle's definition of drama is dependent on some knowledge of his other works. This is particularly true in regard to his notion of the duality of form, a perception which is related to his metaphysical system. Aristotle saw dramatic form as an image of a reality revealing both ideal and material properties.

seeks to project within the structural frame of the theatre that which is permanent, unchanging, and total, and to establish its relationship to that which is fleeting, transitory, and fragmentary.

This motive—the imitation of reality—engenders complexities which are self-evident. Francis Fergusson in his study *The Idea of a Theater* [5] has written that such a function ties drama to the process of human understanding. Fergusson, like Erich Auerbach, suggests that form is not wholly a matter of individual creation. While it may to some extent mirror the imagination of the individual artist, it is perhaps more truly an image of universal perception—the projection of a distinctive world view. An examination of the history of Western theatre would seem to give credence to this interpretation. For the history of the theatre offers extensive documentation of the relationship of the drama to the changing pattern of life. Western forms vary, in this instance from Eastern kinds, many of which appear to have maintained, over a period of centuries, their ancient identities. Western drama, on the contrary, has been characterized by constant change, by a pattern of development as variable as the Western perception of reality. While each epoch has shared with preceding periods some of the perspectives which are the legacy of human knowledge, each period has defined reality in a way that has been peculiar to its own time. Thus, each new concept of drama has reflected something of the past. Each form, however, has adapted a residue of traditional elements in

5. Francis Fergusson, *The Idea of a Theater* (Princeton, 1949). Fergusson attributes aspects of his concept of form to Erich Auerbach and to Kenneth Burke, both of whom interpret form, in neo-Kantian terms, as the imitation of meaning. A look at recent definitions of form would seem to suggest that many twentieth-century aestheticians share the Kantian notion of form as an image of individual knowing. However, theorists differ as to which faculty of knowing art imitates. The irrationalists believe art to be the imitation of understanding; they hold that its origin is in sense impressions. Other twentieth-century schools of criticism are concerned with form as the concretion of objective schemata—the image of the process of reason. Positivist aestheticians find form to be the projection of linguistic schemes, the imitation of a process of naming.

a new and distinctive arrangement. In this sense, form is the projection of human understanding into sensible shape; it is a momentary union of traditional meanings and individual discoveries.[6]

For many reasons, perhaps the basic interpretation of form in the drama is yet that of Aristotle. In the *Poetics,* Aristotle posited a definition which still appears to be fundamental to the understanding of dramatic intent. He described form as an imaginative reconstruction of reality, as an image of human understanding. According to this view, the history of the drama can be interpreted as a moving picture of dynamic forms, as a progression of fictions which develop from simple and naïve impressions to sophisticated and complex ideas. In his *Poetics,* Aristotle traced the development of the dynamic form called "tragedy":

> But when Tragedy and Comedy came to light, the two classes of poets still followed their natural bent: the lampooners became writers of Comedy, and the Epic poets were succeeded by Tragedians, since the drama was a larger and higher form of art.
>
> Whether Tragedy has yet perfected its proper types or not; and whether it is to be judged in itself, or in relation also to the audience,—this raises another question. Be that as it may, Tragedy—as also Comedy—was at first mere improvisation. The one originated with the authors of the Dithyramb, the other with those of the phallic songs, which are still in use in many of our cities. Tragedy advanced by slow degrees; each new element that showed itself was in turn developed. Having passed through many changes, it found its natural form, and there it stopped.[7]

Aristotle interpreted drama as an attempt to reconstruct the essential conditions of human action. The *Poetics* interprets tragedy as a kind of philosophic exploration. Like philosophy, the tragic form is concerned not only with reproducing the

6. See Herbert Read, *The Philosophy of Modern Art* (New York, 1952), pp. 3–14.

7. Butcher, pp. 17, 19.

necessary conditions affecting human action but also with determining the significance of such action in the moral universe. Unlike philosophy, however, tragedy's estimate of the human situation is not reducible to the spare syntax of logic. Instead, it projects an image of moral conflict into the ambiguous language of theatre: into plot, character, dialogue, thought, lyric, and scene. Tragic form thus represents an attempt to mediate between the universal and the particular, to reconcile the unyielding laws of the moral universe with the dynamics of existence in a kingdom of living things. This concept of form, like the contemporary idea, embraces conflict as a principle; for it looks, on the one hand, to a static universe of absolutes, and on the other, to a dynamic world of existences. It is perhaps because of this duality that Aristotle's concept of drama seems today more relevant to the discussion of form in the contemporary theatre than do those of his Renaissance and Augustan followers, many of whom interpreted drama as static structure. The differences between the neo-Aristotelians and their master may in large part be traced to their divergences from his critical method.

Because Aristotle was a scientist as well as a philosopher, he based his idea of form on sense data as well as on abstract reasoning. Since tragedy as a sensible form showed a wide range of mutations, he devised a definition that could accommodate variability. Like the modern positivists, Aristotle seems not to have formulated a closed definition, but rather to have cited an open concept based on a significant distribution of recurrent characteristics. For Aristotle, *Oedipus the King* in effect corresponded to the tragic mode; that is, it represented that point along a continuum where the highest incidence of like characteristics occurred.[8] In his discussion of this work,

8. Morris Weitz offers such a theory of definitions in his essay "The Role of Theory in Aesthetics" in *The Journal of Aesthetics*, XV (September, 1956), 27–35. Weitz credits much of the supporting philosophy underlying his theory to the philosopher Ludwig Wittgenstein.

however, he explored other relevant possibilities. It is interesting to observe a fact that demonstrates the flexibility of Aristotle's thinking: he did not fear, apparently, that the presence of practices divergent from his conclusions served to invalidate his generalization. On the contrary, his citation of mutations seems to have supported the validity of his dynamic theory of form. Although he admired the technique of Sophocles, he wrote of the practice of Euripides: "And Euripides, faulty though he may be in the general management of his subject, yet is felt to be the most tragic of the poets." [9]

The form which Aristotle described was in an important sense an image of philosophic exploration. The works in which he was primarily interested, *Oedipus the King* and *Antigone,* express—in common with the Platonic dialogues—a profound concern about the reconciliation of materiality and ideality. Aristotle recorded that this conflict, treated in some manner by all three of the major Greek dramatists, was most effectively presented in *Oedipus the King*. He commended Sophocles on the particulars of his technique in giving the tragic dilemma sensible form: on the suspenseful quality of his narration; the nobility of his protagonist; the eloquence of his reasoning; the elegance of his style; the universality of his myth; and the restraint of his staging. After an extended discussion of the genre, Aristotle made the following generalization about the tragic form: "Tragedy, then, is an imitation of an action that is serious, complete, and of a certain magnitude; in language embellished with each kind of artistic ornament, the several kinds being found in separate parts of the play; in the form of action, not of narrative; through pity and fear effecting the proper purgation of these emotions." [10]

The *Poetics* does not appear to have been intended as a closed definition of dramatic form. It may be described, rather, as the exposition of an open concept, as an attempt to illumine a work

9. Butcher, p. 47.
10. *Ibid.*, p. 23.

which Aristotle believed to have represented the highest point of development in a mature genre. The primary validity of Aristotle's definition of the form of Sophoclean tragedy still seems to rest in a less scientific attribute, to reside in a quality which may be described as "illumination." For his essay remains a poetic statement about the nature of the dramatic form: it is itself an image of an image of reality.

Since the decline of the Greek theatre, there have been three major adjustments in Aristotle's concept of form. Neoclassicism, romanticism, and realism may be interpreted as formal variations upon the classic principle of imitation. A careful look at these three developments would seem to confirm Fergusson's observation that the variable factor in form is the changing face of reality. The first of these revolutions in perspective may be seen in the neoclassic drama of ancient Rome. The Roman drama, unlike the ambiguous form of Greek tragedy, was conceived as an image of human action in a material world—as an exploration of those natural phenomena which Aristotle believed to have been only the face of ultimate reality. Neoclassicism thus restricted the conditions of imitation.

The neoclassic form, writes Francis Fergusson, may be described as the "rational imitation of human action." [11] Although the Stoic philosopher Seneca provided what is perhaps the chief example of this form, the vitality of the neoclassic concept must be traced to the influence of its chief theorist, the poet Horace. As George Saintsbury has pointed out, it has been primarily the Horatian definition of form which has determined the course of Western criticism.[12] It was Horace who provided the theatre with most of its often-invoked "rules."

A comparative study of the treatises of Aristotle and Horace

11. Fergusson, p. 48.

12. George Saintsbury, *A History of Criticism* (Edinburgh, 1900–1904), II, 228.

may serve to document certain critical differences between classic and neoclassic concepts of form. Aristotle's interest in the ideal form—particularly in its poetic mystery—still serves to distinguish his work from that of his Roman successor. The Roman concept attempted to divest tragedy of its metaphysical implications. Horace, taking his point of departure from works such as Seneca's *Oedipus,* concerned himself with the materialistic form of the drama—with its conformity to pre-established standards of order.

Horace is only one of a group of Roman critics who have exercised a major influence on the course of Western drama. Just as Horace was to affect the subsequent definitions of form offered by Western critics, so Seneca would shape dramatic structure; Cicero, rhetoric; Virgil, the art of poetry; and Vitruvius, the art of scene design. The continuing appeal of Roman criticism for later theorists seems to be related to the ability of its writers to reduce complex ideas to logical structures, to give reality a reasonable form. Horace himself commented on the difference between Roman and Hellenic faculties: "To the Greeks the Muse gave native wit, to the Greeks she gave speech in well-rounded phrase; they craved naught but glory. Our Romans, by many a long sum, learn in childhood to divide the *as* into a hundred parts." [13]

Horace's arithmetic figures are significant, for the Latin critic addressed himself to exactly this task: that of computing dramatic structure. Where Aristotle had been concerned with inner form—the essence of organic life—Horace attempted to discern external structure, the logical interrelationship of measurable parts. His discussion of the practice of playwriting is specific, detailed, and wholly discursive in nature; his instructions to the aspiring dramatist are as exact as those of a master engineer. He admonishes his pupil: "Now hear what I, and with me the public, expect. If you want an approving hearer,

13. Horace *The Art of Poetry,* trans. H. Rushton Fairclough in *Horace* (London, 1926), p. 477.

one who waits for the curtain, and will stay in his seat till the singer cries 'Give your applause,' you must note the manners of each age, and give a befitting tone to shifting natures and their years."[14]

Horace proposed to substitute for the metaphorical form of the Greeks a drama related to the exploration of practical problems incident to everyday life in a bourgeois society. In his *Art of Poetry* he proposed a new concept of organicism in the drama, a unity based on congruity of parts and on agreeable effect. He describes this sensibility—this taste for surface refinement:

> If a painter chose to join a human head to the neck of a horse, and to spread feathers of many a hue over limbs picked up now here now there, so that what at the top is a lovely woman ends below in a black and ugly fish, could you, my friends, if favoured with a private view, refrain from laughing? Believe me, dear Pisos, quite like such pictures would be a book, whose idle fancies shall be shaped like a sick man's dreams, so that neither head nor foot can be assigned to a single shape. "Painters and poets," you say, "have always had an equal right in hazarding anything." We know it: this licence we poets claim and in our turn we grant the like; but not so far that savage should mate with tame, or serpents couple with birds, lambs with tigers.[15]

It is because of its fundamental interest in the material world that the neoclassic definition remains relevant to the explication of later forms of drama. Greek tragedy, while expressing concern for phenomenal reality, did not attribute to it ultimate value. On the contrary, it assigned ultimate meaning to the static and eternal universe of the ideal. The elevation of material existence to a plane of first importance was the contribution of the neoclassicists. Roman drama was to bequeath this concept of form as a legacy to modern European theatre. It was to dominate the French and English theatres of the seventeenth century, and to maintain its life in European theatre throughout the eighteenth and nineteenth centuries. While it had its

14. *Ibid.*, p. 463.
15. *Ibid.*, p. 451.

most successful realization in the tragedy of seventeenth-century France, it has continued to affect the shape of the drama to this day.

The rise of romanticism marked a second major revolution in the concept of form in Western drama. For if neoclassicism modified the form of Aristotelian description by constriction, romanticism altered the conditions of imitation by reason of extension. Romanticism expanded the Aristotelian universe by adding a third mode of reality: human consciousness. Aristotle noted this "inner circumstance" briefly. Perhaps because of the influence of Plato, he warned against emphasis on the irrational in the drama. Romanticism not only sought to recover this subjective plane to art, it attempted to establish such "inner circumstance" as the ground of ultimate meaning.

It is customary in literary studies to date the rise of the romantic world view to a time near the beginning of the eighteenth century. Insofar as the theatre is concerned, however, this date must be altered. For while romantic theory is in large measure the contribution of the eighteenth and nineteenth centuries, romantic drama—as an original form—completed its cycle of development somewhat earlier. Theatrical romanticism is in actuality the creation of the Renaissance. It grew out of problems intensified by the age. The Renaissance artist, faced with the sharp contradictions of opposing world views, attempted to reconcile the contrary claims of medievalism and classicism by the construction of a more complex concept of reality—consciousness. Francis Fergusson notes that this romantic image was rendered by a number of non-dramatic writers: particularly by Dante, Cervantes, and John Milton.[16]

Insofar as the history of the drama is concerned, there is little doubt that the chief architect of the romantic form remains William Shakespeare. It was Shakespeare who articulated the universe that was to provide the poets, dramatists, and theorists

16. See Francis Fergusson's *Dante's Drama of the Mind* (Princeton, 1953).

of the eighteenth and nineteenth centuries with their definition of form. In his tragedies as well as in many of his comedies, Shakespeare shaped the plural reality of romantic description. In *Hamlet, Macbeth,* and *King Lear,* for example, phenomenal reality is mirrored simultaneously in an interior world of subjective response and in an outer universe of static truth. The actions of Hamlet, Lear, and Macbeth as well as those of Shylock, Leontes, and Prospero are interpreted on the multidimensional stage of human consciousness. Because of the nature of his pluralistic universe, the actions of Shakespeare's characters assume infinitely greater complexity than those of Sophocles or Seneca. In both classic and neoclassic forms, the protagonist is charged with the responsibility of determining the significance of his actions. In the romantic drama, the very complexity of reality aggravates the conflict. "How am I to know?" is the anguished cry of the romantic protagonist Hamlet. The play itself is an attempt to answer this critical question.

The concept of form which emerged in the writings of the romantic theorists of the eighteenth and nineteenth centuries must be considered as retrospective in nature. The dramatic theories of Friedrich von Schiller, Johann Wolfgang von Goethe, the brothers August and Friedrich von Schlegel, as well as those of Georg W. F. Hegel and Friedrich Nietzsche, do not represent so much the formulation of new concepts of form as they do the reconstruction of the laws underlying the earlier work of Shakespeare, Corneille, Lope, Dante, Cervantes, Milton, and others. These principles, applied to the great reservoir of Northern myth and feeling, were to produce the late "romantic" drama of Goethe, Schiller, Victor Hugo, and Richard Wagner. Because of the distinctive genius of its playwrights, the romantic drama of the eighteenth and nineteenth centuries did not retain a purely imitative quality. On the contrary, the concepts borrowed from the Renaissance were given new character by the introduction of original materials from native grounds.

It seems correct to say that the theatrical romanticism of the eighteenth and nineteenth centuries was important primarily because of its success in recovering the principles which had undergirded the vision of late Renaissance dramatists such as Shakespeare. The discussions of Hegel, Nietzsche, and Wagner are of particular value in interpreting specific aspects of this mode of imitation. However, the most important theorist, insofar as the description of the romantic universe is concerned, is a philosopher who is not primarily associated with dramatic theory. If the dramatic form of Shakespeare pictured a universe possessing multiple modes of being and action, it was in the metaphysics of Immanuel Kant that this complex structure was given philosophic verification.

As Aristotelian metaphysics delimited the reality of classical description, so Kantian metaphysics defined the reality against which the romantic protagonist's actions were projected. Indeed, Kant on philosophic ground explored those same questions which haunted Hamlet, Lear, and Macbeth: What is the nature of reality? How may we know it? What is the ground of being? How may we verify it? What is morality? How may moral values be determined? Kant's great service to drama and to modern dramatic criticism was his systematization of the complex reality of romantic perception. Although he raised again essentially unanswerable questions, he offered to the drama—and indeed to the arts in general—philosophic support for an increasingly complex perception of human action. Moreover, he provided for romanticism a verification of its own poetic perception of truth by defining consciousness in essentially creative terms. Kant described cognition as a creative process of connecting the separate facets of experience—a process that makes effective use of the synthetic power of the imagination. In his *Critique of Aesthetic Judgment*[17] he described form in these essentially romantic terms:

The poet ventures to realise to sense, rational Ideas of invisible beings, the kingdom of the blessed, hell, eternity, creation, etc.; or, even if he

17. Immanuel Kant, *Critique of Aesthetic Judgment,* trans. James Creed Meredith (Oxford, 1911).

deals with things of which there are examples in experience,—e.g. death, envy and all vices, also love, fame, and the like,—he tries, by means of Imagination, which emulates the play of Reason in its quest after a maximum, to go beyond the limits of experience and to present them to Sense with a completeness of which there is no example in nature. It is, properly speaking, in the art of the poet, that the faculty of aesthetical Ideas can manifest itself in its full measure.[18]

Kant's concept of poetic creation shows marked similarities to that of the romantic poet and critic Samuel Taylor Coleridge. Both ascribed to affective reality the shape of human consciousness. Both conceived form to be the image of a complex process of perception.[19] In his writings, Coleridge abandoned the narrow neoclassic definition favored by critics such as John Dryden. The form he described was rather the imitation of total consciousness, the reconstruction of the intricate process of knowing. In the following passage, Coleridge echoes Kant's discussion of the synthetic properties of the subjective power of imagination:

This leads us to what the drama should be. And first, it is not *a copy* of nature; but it is an imitation. This is the universal principle of the fine arts. . . . Suffice it [to say] that one great principle is common to all, a principle which probably is the condition of all consciousness, without which we should feel and imagine only by discontinuous moments, and be plants or animals instead of men. I mean that ever-varying balance, or balancing, of images, notions, or feelings (for I avoid the vague word, idea) conceived as in opposition to each other; in short, the perception of identity and contrariety, the least degree of which constitutes *likeness,* the greatest absolute difference; but the infinite gradations between these two form all the play and all the interest of our intellectual and moral being, till it lead us to a feeling and an object more awful than it seems to me compatible with even the present subject to utter aloud, tho' [I am] most desirous to suggest it. For there alone are all things at once differ-

18. *Kant: Selections,* ed. Theodore Meyer Greene (New York, 1929), p. 427. The translation of this passage by J. H. Bernard is somewhat more readable than that of Meredith, p. 176.

19. The question of Coleridge's dependence on theorists such as Kant and August Wilhelm Schlegel is not quite clear. It seems likely, however, that he arrived independently at many of the same ideas formulated by the German philosophers.

ent and the same; there alone, as [in] the principle of all things does distinction exist unaided by division—will and reason, succession of time and unmoving eternity, infinite change and ineffable rest.[20]

The romantic definition, the most complex of the ideas of form which, by the nineteenth century, had emerged in Western theatre, attempted to reconcile the conflicting claims of classicism, neoclassicism, and medievalism within the structural frame of the drama. Romantic writers and theorists, finding that they no longer had recourse to many of the systems, beliefs, and perceptions of the past, were forced to seek new means of giving to individual existence some sense of unity and harmony. Faced with the appearance of irreconcilable conflict in the external world, the romantic dramatist turned to the verification of knowing, to the individual capacity for unifying reality within the consciousness.

Realism, like neoclassicism, is a theory which interprets dramatic form as the reconstruction of objective phenomena rather than as the image of a reality of subjective or transcendental description. Both neoclassic and realist forms are highly humanistic concepts of the drama; each is concerned with that world of experience in which man alone has ultimate power. But if neoclassicism employed reason as the chief instrumentation of its investigative technique, the realists attempted to document human action by empirical means—that is, by means of scientific data.[21]

Historically, realism emerged in reaction to a third massive revolution in human understanding. It was the response of the theatre to the age of science. There had been, prior to the nineteenth century, some evidence of the realistic bias in Western theatre, especially in the drama of Euripides and in that of the

20. Samuel Taylor Coleridge, Notes on "Dramatic Illusion" in *Coleridge's Shakespearean Criticism,* ed. Thomas Middleton Raysor (Cambridge, Mass., 1936), I, 204–5.

21. See John Howard Lawson, *Theory and Technique of Playwriting* (New York, 1936), pp. 158–287.

New Comedy writer Menander. Similarly, realistic detail was a characteristic of the medieval drama, although its use was seldom systematic in application or coherent in effect. Such detail was evident also in the English drama of the Jacobean period, and it became an important element of technique in the theatre of the eighteenth century. Perhaps the earliest example of English dramatic literature which may justifiably be assigned to the realist tradition is George Lillo's bougeois tragedy: *The London Merchant.* Certainly, realistic techniques have been used in all epochs of history. It was, however, in the nineteenth century that this idea of form gained a mode of verification for its image of material reality. The rise of the sciences of human behavior—psychology, sociology, and political science—gave added impetus to this view of imitation. For if the romantic theorists found their epistemology in the metaphysics of Kant, the dramatists in the realist tradition adapted their theories of knowledge from the doctrines of Auguste Comte, Herbert Spencer, Karl Marx, and Sigmund Freud.

Historical realism attempted to interpret human action in the language of the biological and sociological sciences. It assumed human actions to be natural phenomena corresponding to the laws governing the biological kingdom. Thus, one of the chief techniques of verification in realism is the quasi-scientific technique described as "naturalism." Naturalism attempts to verify reality by the massive accumulation of sense data. While most dramatists in the realist tradition have employed this method of validation, the bias of theatrical realism-naturalism has varied. For example, it may be noted that some of the work of Chekhov may be described as "psychological naturalism." Gorky's perspective, on the other hand, was sociopolitical in nature, while Strindberg employed the language of Darwin.[22]

It now seems correct to associate the formal beginning of realism-naturalism with Eugène Scribe (1791-1861), the theorist

22. See August Strindberg, "Author's Foreword to *Miss Julie*" in *Six Plays of Strindberg,* trans. Elizabeth Sprigge (Garden City, New York, 1955), pp. 61–73.

of the well-made play. For Scribe, in revolt against the excesses of romanticism, codified the quasi-scientific approach which was to serve more gifted artists such as Ibsen. It was Scribe—not Ibsen—who developed the methodological apparatus of the realistic drama: the well-made play. His form represented an attempt to apply the scientific method to the traditional subject matter of the theatre. The thesis drama, popularized by Augier, by Ibsen, and by George Bernard Shaw, merely clothed the well-made play in more literary language and with more philosophically oriented contents.

Despite association with playwrights such as Ibsen, Shaw, and John Galsworthy, the realist-naturalist form seems to have reached its technical maturity in the work of two less gifted writers, in that of Henri Becque (1837–1899) and Eugène Brieux (1858–1932). An examination of the masterpieces of Ibsen, Chekhov, Tolstoy, Shaw, Strindberg, Synge, and others shows that these more talented dramatists, while professing theoretical allegiance to the realist tradition, in practice reflected serious divergences from its concept of form. Today, plays such as *Ghosts, The Cherry Orchard, The Power of Darkness, Saint Joan, Miss Julie,* and *The Playboy of the Western World* are only superficially acceptable as examples of the realist-naturalist form. Indeed, even often-cited examples, such as *The Lower Depths,* are not devoid of anti-realist tendencies.

The post-romantic playwright Maurice Maeterlinck, an architect of the revolt against realism, commented on this phenomenon in an essay on the poetic in the drama. Maeterlinck observed that the work of the great dramatists of the realistic era transcended the limitations of the form.[23] A study of the masterpieces written between 1850 and 1900 shows that Maeterlinck was essentially correct in his observation. In the same way as Shakespeare, Corneille, and Wagner seemed to find beneath external events a more enduring reality, so Chekhov, Strind-

23. Maurice Maeterlinck, Preface to *Plays* (Theatre I), trans. Barrett Clark, in *European Theories of the Drama* (rev. ed.; New York, 1947), p. 415.

berg, Tolstoy, and Ibsen—in certain of their works—evolved an essentially poetic method which they have bequeathed to contemporary dramatists such as Tennessee Williams. They discovered beneath the surface of natural life a system of truths no less universal than classical, neoclassical, and romantic "laws" had been. Moreover, these poetic realists were able to use the quasi-scientific knowledges of the nineteenth century as external signs of this universal meaning. Strindberg wrote that he employed Darwin's theory of heredity as a symbol of fate. Similarly, Tolstoy and Chekhov were to use class conflict as a sign of persistent human struggle, and Ibsen was to see in an industrialized Europe a parallel to the moral dilemma of ancient Athens.

Orthodox realism proved too narrow a doctrine for the explication of the complex world of the twentieth century. Realism gained its most spectacular success as a technique for the control of the art of the *mise en scène.* But even in this case it proved restricting and came to be modified sharply in the direction of the poetic. The great *metteur en scène* Konstantin Stanislavsky modified his realistic method for the production of Chekhovian drama. And it was the pre-expressionist designer Gordon Craig who was to give to Ibsen's *Pretenders* an appropriate interpretation. Today it is debatable whether realism has established itself as a significant form. It seems certain that it has gained a permanent place in the theatre as a technique, but its major achievement seems to have been corrective in nature. It eliminated certain excesses associated with the subjective form, romanticism, and with the more abstract forms, classicism and neoclassicism. Certainly realism succeeded in establishing in naturalism a new basis for measuring validity in art, and in consequence forged a new link with life itself. To this extent, its method has become a permanent part of Western theatrical technique.

While the realistic definition was clear, systematic, and useful, the work of great dramatists in the epoch of its domination did not actually conform to many of its prerequisites. Their tendency to idealization alienated them from realism and propelled them more and more toward poetic abstraction. Plays such as *Rosmersholm* (1886), *The Master Builder* (1892), *The Dream Play* (1902), *The Cherry Orchard* (1904), and *Saint Joan* (1923) were but a step from the early experiments of the contemporary period and the revolutionary technique known as expressionism.

The formal beginning of contemporary theatre may be found in European expressionism. Expressionism, one of the most frequently used terms in modern theatrical criticism, is a difficult concept to define. To begin with, it does not appear to designate a form, but rather it signifies the experimental and methodological phases of growth toward a new kind of drama. Since the end of its initial period of experimentalism, a period which ended in the middle-to-late twenties, expressionism seems to have experienced a second and perhaps even a third phase of growth which have been concerned with the synthesis of its experimental techniques. The term "expressionism," therefore, is used by many critics to identify the whole body of anti-realist drama written since 1880. Such writers describe as expressionistic the transitional drama of Ibsen, Strindberg, Gerhart Hauptmann, and Frank Wedekind, as well as some of the work of Chekhov, Shaw, Arthur Pinero, and Oscar Wilde. Other historians classify as expressionist the symbolist drama of Maeterlinck, Paul Claudel, and William Butler Yeats as well as the Dadaist experiments of Guillaume Apollinaire, Alfred Jarry, Jean Cocteau, and Pablo Picasso. Still others apply this term to the contemporary drama of O'Neill, Wilder, Saroyan, Miller, and Williams.

The term "expressionism" was first used as a descriptive title for a new kind of painting concerned with the representation of the reality of inner experience.[24] Expressionism thus shares with romanticism an interest in individual consciousness. But

24. Bernard S. Myers, *The German Expressionists* (New York, 1957), pp. 35–40.

if expressionist reality is partially romantic in kind, it represents a romanticism in which the image of reality has undergone further disintegration. Expressionism differs from romanticism in that it does not suggest that there is within reality a principle of order. On the contrary, expressionism hopes to create, through art, forms which possess a greater unity than that apprehensible in reality itself.

Expressionism grew out of the political, intellectual, and spiritual upheaval of the late nineteenth and early twentieth centuries. By 1900 it had become apparent that industrialization had bequeathed to Western man, along with its benefits, even more complex social, economic, political, and spiritual problems than those which had existed formerly. Expressionist works such as Georg Kaiser's *Gas* (1918 and 1920), Ernst Toller's *Man and the Masses* (1920–21), or Brecht's *Drums in the Night* (1922) reflected the common concerns of the early twentieth century: a fear of machine domination, an acute anxiety about the possibility of physical, spiritual, intellectual, and psychological annihilation, and a revolutionary drive toward social, political, and economic reforms. These comprehensive fears and anxieties, rational and irrational alike, were transmitted without disguise into all of the arts, but particularly into the art of theatre.

The expressionists attempted to restore to the theatre its concern about the nature of human destiny. Like the Greeks, these dramatists proposed to use the theatre as the instrument of their exploration. But if the expressionists wished to return to the primary motivation of Greek drama, they did not seek to recover all of the particulars of tragic form. Indeed, the techniques and theories of the early expressionists were highly eclectic. The systematization of their individual patterns of response into more highly organized modes of expression seems to have begun in the plastic arts. Historians trace the development of theoretical expressionism to the group of European artists known as *Die Brücke*.[25] This group of transitional

25. Herbert Read, *A Concise History of Modern Painting* (New York, 1959), pp. 52–66.

artists, including Edvard Munch, Ernst Ludwig Kirchner, and Emil Nolde, attempted at the turn of the century to bridge the gulf between the world of realist interpretation and these new and revolutionary perspectives in much the same manner as did dramatists such as Wedekind, Strindberg, and—on occasion—Ibsen.[26] These "subjective" expressionists attempted to infuse into realistic and naturalistic forms a quality of inner life with which artists in the twentieth century have remained concerned. They were succeeded in 1907 or 1908 by a dissentient group which included Wassily Kandinsky and Franz Marc. It was these *Blaue Reiter* expressionists who evolved broad theories of form, applicable not only to painting, but—they hoped—to the whole range of artistic expression in the twentieth century.

Near the end of World War I, expressionism moved into what now appears to have been the final phase of its theoretical development. In 1919, the celebrated Bauhaus School was established by the architect Walter Gropius (an expatriate from the Blue Rider group), by Wassily Kandinsky, and by the painter and theorist Paul Klee.[27] The Bauhaus School, originally established at Weimar, was relocated by the government in 1925 and it continued to exist until 1933. It was during this later period that expressionism entered a final period of systematization which was to lead toward a more abstract symbolism. While these more abstract expressionists engaged in many kinds of experimentation, they were ultimately to contribute a highly systematized visual language to the development of the contemporary arts—a catalogue of abstract symbols intended to connote the full range of human understanding.[28]

The activity of the Bauhaus School was particularly important to the development of contemporary drama, not only because of its attempt to establish an international aesthetic

26. Myers, pp. 31, 35, 36, 93, 115.

27. See the discussion of expressionism by Umbro Apollonio in *The Encyclopedia of World Art* (New York, 1961), V, 311–23.

28. See Oskar Schlemmer and others, *The Theatre of the Bauhaus,* trans. Arthur Wensinger (Middletown, Connecticut, 1961).

language but also because of its insistence that such a language should be common to all artistic forms. The Bauhaus envisioned not only an "abstract" art of painting, sculpture, and architecture, but also a theatre of the abstract, an architectonic form described in its manifesto as "total drama." The activity of artists in the Bauhaus, however, was not singular, for in the theatre itself many of the same ideas had developed. Wagner's associate, the Swiss designer Adolphe Appia, had moved his own scenic forms toward greater abstraction.[29] Similarly, the English designer Gordon Craig, concerned with stripping away superfluous detail from the production of Shakespeare, had evolved a theory of visual form roughly comparable to that of German expressionists.

The movement of the contemporary form into a second stage of its growth took place as a result of the transplantation of expressionistic themes, techniques, and theories into new cultural environments.[30] The proliferation of expressionistic patterns may be seen in the history of the theatre between the great wars. Luigi Pirandello was one of the first dramatists in this second generation of writers. *Six Characters in Search of an Author* (1921) is a blend of theoretical expressionism and the native tradition of Goldoni and the *commedia dell' arte*. In the same way, a new type of theatre emerged out of the union of expressionism and French classicism. This synthesis was to produce plays such as Paul Claudel's *The Satin Slipper* (1919–1924), André Obey's *Noah* (1931), and Jean Cocteau's *The Infernal Machine* (1934). In Britain, expressionism produced modifications in traditional forms, especially in the history play. Plays such as *Saint Joan* (1923), *Murder in the Cathedral* (1935), and Christopher Fry's *The Boy with a Cart* (1937) are examples of this synthesis.

Two new types of drama emerged out of this creative period. The activity of Bertolt Brecht resulted in a new kind of cryptic

29. Adolphe Appia, "The Future of Production," in *Theatre Arts Anthology*, ed. Rosamond Gilder and others (New York, 1950), pp. 519–33.

30. See Huntly Carter, *The New Spirit in the European Theatre* (London, 1925).

comedy, not unlike cartoons. Plays such as *The Threepenny Opera* (1928), *The Good Woman of Setzuan* (1938–40), and *Mother Courage* (1939) seemed to restore to the modern theatre the lost art of satirical drama.[31] In his brilliant theatrical essays on life in the twentieth century, Brecht launched the kind of virulent attack on humanity formerly displayed in Aristophanic comedy. A second type of drama was oriented in a different direction. The American theatre of Eugene O'Neill, Elmer Rice, John Howard Lawson, Thornton Wilder, and Paul Green employed expressionism as an instrument of a more tragically oriented exploration—as a way of discovering ultimate meaning in the fabric of American life. *The Emperor Jones* (1920) and *The Hairy Ape* (1922), like Elmer Rice's *The Adding Machine* (1923), John Howard Lawson's *Processional* (1925), Thornton Wilder's *Our Town* (1938), and others, were the evidence of a new kind of theatre which resulted from the application of expressionistic techniques to indigenous American themes.

By 1945, the shape of the maturing contemporary form could be distinguished from the earlier experiments of its expressionist innovators. The gradual synthesis of expressionism with both popular and traditional kinds had broadened the range of themes, techniques, and linguistic structures which appeared in the emerging contemporary form. Perhaps a more important development was a shift in emphasis from the immediate conflicts within Western societies to problems common to the whole of the human race.

Today it seems clear that a fifth major cycle of development has begun in twentieth-century Western theatre; we are witnessing a revolution that has produced a kind of drama which, in its total aspect, is neither classical, neoclassical, romantic, nor realistic. At mid-century, this new dramatic kind seemed to have reached a third stage of its growth. By 1945, this revolutionary impulse had produced three generations of dramatists

31. See Martin Esslin's discussion of German expressionism in *Bertolt Brecht: A Choice of Evils* (London, 1959), pp. 21–53.

and a significant body of dramatic literature. More important, it had created a vital, popular form specifically related to the interpretation of reality in the twentieth century. What is the nature of this twentieth-century drama? What are the characteristic elements of its form? In succeeding chapters, I shall attempt to answer this question through the consideration of a significant example in the contemporary pattern: the drama of the American playwright Tennessee Williams.

chapter two

WILLIAMS AND THE LYRIC MOMENT

And so it was I entered the broken world
To trace the visionary company of love, its voice
An instant in the wind (I know not whither hurled)
But not for long to hold each desperate choice.

This quotation from the American poet Hart Crane is the epigraph with which Tennessee Williams introduces the play often judged as his masterwork. In these lines, which are inscribed on the frontispiece of *A Streetcar Named Desire,* Williams provides an appropriate point of departure for a discussion of his idea of form. For the words embody a concept of artistic imitation, an appropriate definition of his form. Williams, like Crane, is concerned with the reality of a "broken world." [1] Form

NOTE: The quotation following the chapter title is from a poem by Hart Crane, "The Broken Tower," which appears in *The Collected Poems of Hart Crane* (New York: Liveright Publishing Corp., 1933), pp. 135–36.

1. In his preface to *Miss Julie* (in *Six Plays of Strindberg,* trans. Elizabeth Sprigge, p. 65), Strindberg gave a similar definition. He wrote: "My souls

in his drama is the imitation of the individual search for a way of redeeming a shattered universe.[2]

Thus Williams may not properly be described as a realist. Both his concept of reality and his mode of imitation reject certain fundamental realist principles. There is greater justification for regarding him as a romantic, for a study of his work shows that his indebtedness to romantic sources—to Shakespeare, Goethe, Wagner, and the symbolist poets of the late nineteenth and early twentieth centuries—is considerable. Moreover, much of Williams' pattern of figuration is romantic in quality, especially in its preoccupation with hallucinatory levels of experience: with gargoyles, monsters, and the dark-in-light patterns which Victor Hugo described as *grotesque*. Williams, who often describes himself as a romantic, is concerned with poetic paradox—with light in dark, good within evil, body against soul, God and Satan. His dramatic form, like that discussed by Hegel, represents the struggle of man to transcend his humanity, to provide for himself a mode of reconciliation with divine purpose.[3] But Williams' form is also of expression-

(characters) are conglomerations of past and present stages of civilization, bits from books and newspapers, scraps of humanity, rags and tatters of fine clothing, patched together as is the human soul."

2. The later expressionists, of course, attempted to create such a symbol from shattered images. Herbert Read describes their synthetic image as "constructive." See his discussion of image-making in *The Philosophy of Modern Art* (New York, 1952), pp. 47–48.

3. Certain elements of Williams' theory parallel those of the romantic aestheticians. See Georg W. F. Hegel, *Lectures on Aesthetics* in *The Philosophy of Hegel,* trans. Bernard Bosanquet and William Bryant (New York, 1953). A particularly pertinent passage reads as follows (p. 358):

"Thus, spiritual reconciliation is to be conceived and represented only as an activity, a movement of the spirit—as a process in the course of which there arises a struggle, a conflict; and the pain, the death, the agony of nothingness, the torment of the spirit and of materiality (*Leiblichkeit*) make their appearance as essential moments or elements. For as, in the next place, God separates or distinguishes (*ausscheidet*) finite actuality from Himself, so also finite man, who begins with himself as outside the divine kingdom, assumes the task of elevating himself to God, of freeing himself from the finite, of doing away with nugatoriness, and of becoming, through this sacrifice (*Ertödten*) of his immediate actuality, that which God, in His appearance as man, has made objective as true actuality."

istic lineage. Like the objective expressionists—notably Wassily Kandinsky—the playwright is concerned with the objectification of subjective vision, with its transformation into concrete symbols.[4] Indeed, one of the most important aspects of Williams' dramaturgy derives from this motive. Like the objective expressionists, the playwright regards art as one of the great life forms, as an instrument of reconciliation no less important than religion, philosophy, politics, or human love.

The search for a concrete expressive form—a shape congruent with poetic vision—is a motif that appears throughout the work of Williams. It is the central theme of *The Glass Menagerie*. Similarly, it is an important aspect of dramatic development in the middle works: *A Streetcar Named Desire, Summer and Smoke, Cat on a Hot Tin Roof, Camino Real,* and *Orpheus Descending*. It is a more obscure element of action in *The Rose Tattoo* and *Sweet Bird of Youth*. In *The Night of the Iguana,* Williams emphasizes again this lyric theme: his search for truth and meaning within the moment of poetic vision. In this late drama he gives expression to the complete cycle of poetic search. He states this theme, shows its development, and arrives at a resolution in the poem which his "Tiresias" finishes, appropriately, at the moment of death. The poem, recited in its entirety at the climax of the play, is here quoted in full:

> How calmly does the orange branch
> Observe the sky begin to blanch
> Without a cry, without a prayer,
> With no betrayal of despair.
>
> Sometime while night obscures the tree
> The zenith of its life will be
> Gone past forever, and from thence
> A second history will commence.
>
> A chronicle no longer gold,
> A bargaining with mist and mould,

4. See, for example, the discussion of this principle in the theory of Paul Klee (*The Inward Vision: Watercolors, Drawings, Writings,* trans. Norbert Guterman [New York, 1958]), pp. 6–10.

And finally the broken stem
The plummeting to earth; and then

An intercourse not well designed
For beings of a golden kind
Whose native green must arch above
The earth's obscene, corrupting love.

And still the ripe fruit and the branch
Observe the sky begin to blanch
Without a cry, without a prayer,
With no betrayal of despair.

O Courage, could you not as well
Select a second place to dwell,
Not only in that golden tree
But in the frightened heart of me?

(Act III, pp. 123–24)

Williams describes his elemental form as "personal lyricism." In an essay called "Person to Person," he defines personal lyricism as "The outcry of prisoner to prisoner from the cell in solitary where each is confined for the duration of his life." [5] The dramatist describes the human condition as a state of metaphysical loneliness. He writes of life,

> It is a lonely idea, a lonely condition, so terrifying to think of that we usually don't. And so we talk to each other, write and wire each other, call each other short and long distance across land and sea, clasp hands with each other at meeting and at parting, fight each other and even destroy each other because of this always somewhat thwarted effort to break through walls to each other. As a character in a play once said, "We're all of us sentenced to solitary confinement inside our own skins."
>
> (Preface to *Cat on a Hot Tin Roof,* p. vi)

Like other contemporaries, Williams perceives in the human condition a constant threat of diminution. He speaks of this corrosive influence in the introduction to *The Rose Tattoo:*

> It is this continual rush of time, so violent that it appears to be screaming, that deprives our actual lives of so much dignity and meaning, and

5. Williams, Preface to *Cat on a Hot Tin Roof,* p. vi. (For full citations of Tennessee Williams' works, see the Appendix.)

it is, perhaps more than anything else, the *arrest of time* which has taken place in a completed work of art that gives to certain plays their feeling of depth and significance. . . . Contemplation is something that exists outside of time, and so is the tragic sense. . . . If the world of a play did not offer us this occasion to view its characters under that special condition of a *world without time,* then, indeed, the characters and occurrences of drama would become equally pointless, equally trivial, as corresponding meetings and happenings in life. (Preface, pp. vi-vii)

It is clear here, as in other instances in the dramatist's critical analyses, that Williams hopes to extract from art a truth greater than that ordinarily apprehensible in life. The central problem of his anti-realist dramaturgy is how to reconstitute felt experience in such a manner as to reveal—or to create—absolute truth.

This problem is explored in the short verse drama, *The Purification*. Here the playwright dramatizes the conflict which the poet experiences as he struggles to give concrete form to vision. In the following lines, the Son, the poet-figure, speaks of his frustration, of the insufficiency of his technique:

The truth?
Why ask me for that?
Ask it of him, the player—
for truth is sometimes alluded to in music.
But words are too loosely woven to catch it in. . .
A bird can be snared as it rises
or torn to earth by the falcon.
His song, which is truth,
is not to be captured ever.
It is an image, a dream,
it is the link to the mother,
the belly's rope that dropped our bodies from God
a longer time ago than we remember!
(In 27 *Wagons Full of Cotton,* p. 40)

But the problem of the lyric form, as defined by Williams, is not merely one of technique. In *Camino Real* he draws a portrait of a poet who has "sold" his art and in consequence lost his power of vision. The decadent "Lord Byron" speaks of the cessation of "celestial music":

—That was my vocation once upon a time, before it was obscured by vulgar plaudits!—Little by little it was lost among gondolas and palazzos!— . . .

. . . .

. . . Oh, I wrote many cantos in Venice and Constantinople and in Ravenna and Rome, on all of those Latin and Levantine excursions that my twisted foot led me into—but I wonder about them a little. They seem to improve as the wine in the bottle—dwindles. . . *There is a passion for declivity in this world!*

And lately I've found myself listening to hired musicians behind a row of artificial palm trees—instead of the single—pure-stringed instrument of my heart. . .

Well, then, it's time to leave here!— . . .

—There is a time for departure even when there's no certain place to go!

I'm going to look for one, now. I'm sailing to Athens. At least I can look up at the Acropolis, I can stand at the foot of it and look up at broken columns on the crest of a hill—if not purity, at least its recollection. . .

I can sit quietly looking for a long, long time in absolute silence, and possibly, yes, *still* possibly—

The old pure music will come to me again. . . .

(Block VIII, pp. 77–78)

In his concept of form, then, Williams recapitulates certain ideas drawn from the romantic tradition. Particularly, he follows the romantics in ascribing to art the ability to mediate between dark drives and luminous truth, between body and soul.[6] Like the romantics, he assigns the function of revelation —the disclosure of absolute knowledge—to the artist. This aspect of his theory of form finds perhaps its most illuminating discussion in the writings of Henri Bergson. Bergson wrote in his famous essay *Laughter:*

6. See Nietzsche, *The Birth of Tragedy* and *The Genealogy of Morals,* trans. Francis Golffing (Garden City, New York, 1956). Williams, like Nietzsche, sees in experience a conflict between the claims of the life force and the impulse toward abstract knowledge.

What is the object of art? Could reality come into direct contact with sense and consciousness, could we enter into immediate communion with things and with ourselves, probably art would be useless, or rather we should all be artists. . . . So art, whether it be painting or sculpture, poetry or music, has no other object than to brush aside the utilitarian symbols, the conventional and socially accepted generalities, in short, everything that veils reality from us, in order to bring us face to face with reality itself.[7]

Hence it follows that art always aims at what is *individual.* What the artist fixes on his canvas is something he has seen at a certain spot, on a certain day, at a certain hour, with a coloring that will never be seen again. What the poet sings of is a certain mood which was his, and his alone, and which will never return. What the dramatist unfolds before us is the life-history of a soul, a living tissue of feelings and events—something, in short, which has once happened and can never be repeated. We may, indeed, give general names to these feelings, but they cannot be the same thing in another soul. They are *individualized.* Thereby, and thereby only, do they belong to art.[8]

Williams conceives drama in such individualized terms. Each of his plays takes the shape of a vision proceeding from the consciousness of the protagonist. In *The Glass Menagerie,* the play represents the memory of the hero, while in *A Streetcar Named Desire* the spectator observes the "Elysian Fields" as it appears to the troubled mind of Blanche. *Cat on a Hot Tin Roof* is approached from the angle of vision belonging to Brick; *Summer and Smoke* through the eyes of Alma; and *Camino Real* through the dreams of Don Quixote. Williams employs varied rationales to account for the angle of distortion in these visions. His interpretative devices—memory, insanity, intoxication, dreams, and death—do not, however, invalidate the acute perception of the protagonist. For, like Shakespeare, Williams seeks to provide a way through which the spectator may be alienated from the "false" world of appearances and induced to share the discovery—or creation—of a world of eternal truth. In the prologue to *The Glass Menagerie,* the poet-figure explains to the spectator: "Yes, I have tricks in my pocket,

7. Henri Bergson, *Laughter* trans. *Cloudesley* Brereton and Fred Rothwell (New York, 1911), pp. 150–57.
8. *Ibid.,* p. 161.

I have things up my sleeve. But I am the opposite of a stage magician. He gives you illusion that has the appearance of truth. I give you truth in the pleasant disguise of illusion."[9] Through the playwright's intermediaries, the "fevered visions" of life pass before the spectator and metamorphose into images embodying a greater meaning than does the experience which they are intended to interpret.

If Williams is indebted to the romantic and postromantic traditions for some aspects of his personal lyricism, there are other factors which differentiate his work from that of earlier dramatists. For he is specifically concerned with the interpretation of those crises—inner and outer—which attend the human condition in the world of today. His basic perspective at this point shows fundamental correspondences to those of other contemporaries. Jean-Paul Sartre, in an essay on the theatre in France, has written that it is the responsibility of the drama to help modern man to discern the ultimate significance of his own life. Sartre contends that it is the specific function of the theatre to provide an appropriate structure for moral exploration, to create a form in which the human dilemma—in its present dimensions—may be given vivid exposition:

> For them [the playwrights] man is not to be defined as a "reasoning animal," or a "social" one, but as a free being, entirely indeterminate, who must choose his own being when confronted with certain necessities, such as being already committed in a world full of both threatening and favorable factors among other men who have made their choices before him, who have decided in advance the meaning of those factors. He is faced with the necessity of having to work and die, of being hurled into a life already complete which yet is his own enterprise and in which he can never have a second chance; where he must play his cards and take risks no matter what the cost. That is why we feel the urge to put on the stage certain situations which throw light on the main aspects of the condition of man and to have the spectator participate in the free choice which man makes in these situations.[10]

9. Scene I, pp. 4–5.
10. Jean-Paul Sartre, "Forgers of Myth," *Theatre Arts*, XXX (June, 1946), 325; reprinted by permission of *Theatre Arts* Magazine.

Williams' comment on this question, though more poetic in its language, nevertheless contains much of the same content:

> The great and only possible dignity of man lies in his power deliberately to choose certain moral values by which to live as steadfastly as if he, too, like a character in a play, were immured against the corrupting rush of time. Snatching the eternal out of the desperately fleeting is the great magic trick of human existence. As far as we know, as far as there exists any kind of empiric evidence, there is no way to beat the game of *being* against *non-being,* in which non-being is the predestined victor on realistic levels. (Preface to *The Rose Tattoo,* p. ix)

Williams and Sartre reflect, in this instance, much the same point of view, a fact which may be traced to the presence of similarities in perspective among all dramatists in the contemporary group. For both the philosophically oriented European drama and the poetically biased American kind share a concept of form as the imitation of a moment of critical insight, a moment alienated from human time. While Sartre presumes the explication and indeed the perception of such a moment to be primarily rational in nature, O'Neill, Saroyan, Miller, and Williams interpret this instant of knowing in more poetic terms. Williams describes the lyric moment, the subject of his poetic vision, in these terms: "In a play, time is arrested in the sense of being confined. By a sort of legerdemain, events are made to remain *events,* rather than being reduced so quickly to mere *occurrences.* The audience can sit back in a comforting dusk to watch a world which is flooded with light and in which emotion and action have a dimension and dignity that they would likewise have in real existence, if only the shattering intrusion of time could be locked out."[11] It is clear that the reality which Williams seeks to imitate does not, in its entirety, correspond to that which appears in the drama of the nineteenth-century romantics. For the drama of Williams is concerned with a far more ambiguous truth.[12]

11. Preface to *The Rose Tattoo,* pp. viii–ix.

12. The playwright articulates some tenets of his system of image-building in the Preface to *Camino Real.*

The romantics, despite their predilection toward revolt, posited an ideal universe which rested on an unmoved power—a power Hegel called "God." Goethe threatened Faust with damnation for his envy of divine power and knowledge. The celebration of a revolutionary individualism in *Sturm und Drang* did not displace the romantic belief in a pre-existent order in the universe. Even Wagner, in his discussion of form, identifies in reality fixed entities such as religion, state, individual, and nature; he defines human experience in terms of ideals such as passion, imagination, and hate.[13] The romantics did not, then, even in their recognition of a dynamic element in experience, deny the presence of an essentially static order in the moral universe. Of the romantics, apparently only Nietzsche could conceive of a truly unsystematized existence. Indeed, Nietzsche, filled with Faustian envy of the Creator, sought to conceive a kind of art which should usurp divine power and create new universes superior to existent forms.

Williams, like Nietzsche, is inclined to challenge the pre-established reality of romantic description. He rejects, moreover, many of the fundamental principles which underlie the romantic theory of image-making. Rather, he is concerned with the creation of an art which is superior to and often in contradiction to known reality. Like the expressionists, Williams regards form as abstraction, as a dynamic structure suspended in metaphysical time and space. He writes of such a form in the preface to *Camino Real:*

> The color, the grace and levitation, the structural pattern in motion, the quick interplay of live beings, suspended like fitful lightning in a cloud, these things are the play, not words on paper, nor thoughts and ideas of an author. . . . (Afterword, p. xii)

> A convention of the play is existence outside of time in a place of no specific locality. . . . (Foreword, p. viii)

13. See Richard Wagner, *Opera and Drama,* trans. Edwin Evans (London, 1913), I, 317–96.

My desire was to give these audiences my own sense of something wild and unrestricted that ran like water in the mountains, or clouds changing shape in a gale, or the continually dissolving and transforming images of a dream. This sort of freedom is not chaos nor anarchy. On the contrary, it is the result of painstaking design, and in this work I have given more conscious attention to form and construction than I have in any work before.... (Foreword, p. ix)

This idea of image-making poses a difficult question which must also be raised in regard to the claims of the expressionists: Can form actually be created? Must not form correspond to some aspect of experience, or to the poet's faculties of knowing? Certainly it would seem logical to suggest that Williams, even in *Camino Real,* has drawn from some phase of experience. The solution to this critical dilemma seems to rest in the playwright's poetic intent. For the images created by Williams are not conceived as copies of any known reality. If there is a nature, a state, an individual, a reality, a truth, or a God in the universe of Williams, it has been derealized. For Williams, reality itself lies shattered. In the fragmentary world of his theatre, new images are pieced together from partialities: they are composed from splinters of broken truths.

The playwright describes this fragmented world imperfectly reflected in his "dark mirror":

For the sins of the world are really only its partialities, its incompletions. . . . A wall that has been omitted from a house because the stones were exhausted . . . —these sorts of incompletions are usually covered up or glossed over by some kind of make-shift arrangements. The nature of man is full of such make-shift arrangements, devised by himself to cover his incompletion. He feels a part of himself to be like a missing wall or a room left unfurnished and he tries as well as he can to make up for it.[14]

Clearly, then, the images which appear in the theatre of Williams are not records of events; nor are they symbols drawn intact from the stream of consciousness. For the playwright has subjected his lyric moment to process. In his theatre, the in-

14. Williams, *Desire and the Black Masseur,* in *One Arm and Other Stories,* p. 85.

stant of vision has been re-created: its image has been enlarged and enhanced.

Williams uses, as the symbolic instrumentation of his image-making, the "eye" of the motion picture camera.[15] His images are composed as by montage; that is, they are made up, after the manner of cinematic technique, by the superimposition of figures one upon the other. This technique, introduced into contemporary literature by James Joyce, appears also in the work of other American dramatists, notably in that of Eugene O'Neill and Thornton Wilder. It has, in addition, been employed by a number of French dramatists, including Apollinaire, Jean Giraudoux, and Paul Claudel, as well as by Picasso, Cocteau, and their friends, in that delightful charade *Parade*.[16] Like these dramatists, Williams uses his camera eye sensitively. With it he is able to arrest time, to focus upon the details of his vision, to emphasize elements of its structural composition, to vary his point of view, and to draw a wide variety of parallels.

An example of this camera technique may be seen in an early play, *This Property Is Condemned,* a cinematographic essay on the life of a deprived child. In this work Williams follows his conventional pattern of articulating a key image. He gives sensible form to the poetic universe of the play:

SCENE: *A railroad embankment on the outskirts of a small Mississippi town on one of those milky white winter mornings peculiar to that part*

15. Many artists, including Hart Crane, have been convinced that there is, operating in contemporary symbol-making, a "machine aesthetic." Williams, like Joyce, Eliot, and Pound—and like plastic artists such as Léger—seems to create such "synthetic" symbols: to invent shapes and forms out of the fusion of organic elements. The great film artist Sergei Eisenstein discussed this technique in modern art. He claimed, for example, that Joyce was aware of using the cinematic technique of montage. See Sergei Eisenstein, *The Film Sense,* trans. Jay Leyda (New York, 1947), p. 17. Arthur Miller also discusses the use of the camera eye in his Introduction to *Collected Plays* (New York, 1957), pp. 23–36.

16. *Parade,* produced in 1917 by Picasso, Cocteau, and Erik Satie, was intended as an example of theatrical montage.

of the country. The air is moist and chill. Behind the low embankment of the tracks is a large yellow frame house which has a look of tragic vacancy. Some of the upper windows are boarded, a portion of the roof has fallen away. The land is utterly flat. In the left background is a billboard that says "GIN WITH JAKE" and there are some telephone poles and a few bare winter trees. The sky is a great milky whiteness: crows occasionally make a sound of roughly torn cloth.

(In 27 *Wagons Full of Cotton,* p. 197)

Here Williams has created an image after the manner of the surrealist painters. In this dream-world, with its death symbols, he places a grotesque figure, the child Willie. He describes her in these words:

The girl Willie is advancing precariously along the railroad track, balancing herself with both arms outstretched, one clutching a banana, the other an extraordinarily dilapidated doll with a frowsy blond wig.

She is a remarkable apparition—thin as a beanpole and dressed in outrageous cast-off finery. She wears a long blue velvet party dress with a filthy cream lace collar and sparkling rhinestone beads. On her feet are battered silver kid slippers with large ornamental buckles. Her wrists and her fingers are resplendent with dimestore jewelry. She has applied rouge to her childish face in artless crimson daubs and her lips are made up in a preposterous Cupid's bow. She is about thirteen and there is something ineluctably childlike and innocent in her appearance despite the makeup. She laughs frequently and wildly and with a sort of precocious, tragic abandon. (Page 197)

It is clear that this world of the play is a carefully devised reconstruction of poetic vision. The playwright is concerned with the evocation of a single image. In the twenty minutes or so which make up the playing time, only one other character appears. When the child departs from the stage, no event has taken place, no changes have been made in her life, no information has been given which was not evident upon her appearance. The play exists only to reveal to the spectator a vision of the distorted world in which the child lives. Each element in the scene has been chosen for its symbolic value. The railroad embankment, with its bare trees and singing crows, is as bereft of humanity as the child—a dilapidated doll. Her attempts to clothe her nakedness with baubles remind us of Shakespeare's Lear.

The dramatist follows this same general pattern of image-making in his longer works. Each of the plays represents an attempt to give exposition to poetic vision. Each play is composed like a poem: the dramatist spins out symbolic figures which are its lyric components. *A Streetcar Named Desire* is composed of eleven theatrical images. *Summer and Smoke* has a like number. *Camino Real* is divided into sixteen scenes. *Orpheus Descending* has nine. Some plays, such as *The Rose Tattoo, Cat on a Hot Tin Roof, Suddenly Last Summer,* and *Sweet Bird of Youth,* do not appear at first glance to be composed of such poetic components. Beneath the apparently continuous flow of action, however, a similar structural design may be found. For Williams, the play is an ordered progression of concrete images, images which together give sensible shape to the lyric moment.

The effectiveness of this technique of explication may be measured by the revisions which the playwright was to make in an early work, *Battle of Angels.* This work, which failed in a professional tryout in 1940, was returned to the stage in 1957 as *Orpheus Descending.* A study of the structural alterations made by Williams is enlightening. The playwright seems to have revised the work by adapting its themes to the more complex method of image-making which he had, by 1945, fully developed. *Orpheus Descending* explores the same themes as did *Battle of Angels.* Moreover, it retains most of the same characters. It does not, however, represent the same quality of imitation. For in *Orpheus Descending* Williams gains dramatic power by allowing his symbols to connote many of the contents to which he gave extended explanation in the earlier work. In this way, many of his observations about the depravity and bestiality of life are absorbed into the text at more tolerable levels of apprehension.

Williams plotted his later version to parallel the legendary account of Orpheus' descent into Hell. He describes the death of his Eurydice—Lady Torrance—in a grotesque fertility ritual, a dance of death in life:

[*In a sort of delirium she thrusts the conical gilt paper hat on her head and runs to the foot of the stairs with the paper horn. She blows the horn over and over, grotesquely mounting the stairs, as* VAL *tries to stop her. She breaks away from him and runs up to the landing, blowing the paper horn and crying out:*] I've won, I've won, Mr. Death, I'm going to bear! [*Then suddenly she falters, catches her breath in a shocked gasp and awkwardly retreats to the stairs. Then turns screaming and runs back down them, her cries dying out as she arrives at the floor level. She retreats haltingly as a blind person, a hand stretched out to* VAL, *as slow, clumping footsteps and hoarse breathing are heard on the stairs. She moans:*]—Oh, God, oh—God. . . . (Scene III, p. 114)

One of the most effective illustrations of Williams' concept of "personal lyricism" is *The Glass Menagerie.* This play, still a favorite of American audiences, players, and critics alike, shows Williams' lyric technique in a lighter tone than does *A Streetcar Named Desire.* Although these plays show differences in textural quality—and in coloration—the architectonic pattern in both is much the same. In *The Glass Menagerie,* as in the later work, Williams has ordered his vision in a clear and highly schematic design. In the opening moments of the play, Tom—the poet-figure—speaks to the audience of the conventions which will be observed as the phantoms of his memory are projected before the spectator:

(MUSIC)

The play is memory.

Being a memory play, it is dimly lighted, it is sentimental, it is not realistic.

In memory everything seems to happen to music. That explains the fiddle in the wings.

I am the narrator of the play, and also a character in it.

The other characters are my mother, Amanda, my sister, Laura, and a gentleman caller who appears in the final scenes.

He is the most realistic character in the play, being an emissary from a world of reality that we were somehow set apart from.

But since I have a poet's weakness for symbols, I am using this character also as a symbol; he is the long delayed but always expected something that we live for. (Scene I, p. 5)

Clearly this play is not a factual record of memory; that is, *The Glass Menagerie* is not "automatic writing." Nor is it a psychological account, the clinical record of days. On the contrary, it is a synthetic image, a vision carefully composed by montage. It is an illusion projected by an imaginary camera eye, turned inward upon the self and backward upon the memory. Like Proust, Williams pieces together his images of the past from the fragments of shattered consciousness. The image which he composes in *The Glass Menagerie* is a figure made of diverse perspectives.[17] In essence, this play represents a recapitulation of the poetic journey. The poet-figure Tom invites the spectator to share with him the task of finding meaning in past experience. His final speech in the play summarizes his grasp of universal truth. As Laura blows out her candle, the poet speaks:

I didn't go to the moon, I went much further—for time is the longest distance between two places—

Not long after that I was fired for writing a poem on the lid of a shoe-box.

I left Saint Louis. I descended the steps of this fire-escape for a last time and followed, from then on, in my father's footsteps, attempting to find in motion what was lost in space—

I traveled around a great deal. The cities swept about me like dead leaves, leaves that were brightly colored but torn away from the branches.

I would have stopped, but I was pursued by something.

It always came upon me unawares, taking me altogether by surprise. Perhaps it was a familiar bit of music. Perhaps it was only a piece of transparent glass—

Perhaps I am walking along a street at night, in some strange city, before I have found companions. I pass the lighted window of a shop where perfume is sold. The window is filled with pieces of colored glass, tiny transparent bottles in delicate colors, like bits of a shattered rainbow.

Then all at once my sister touches my shoulder. I turn around and look into her eyes. . .

Oh, Laura, Laura, I tried to leave you behind me, but I am more faithful than I intended to be!

17. *The Glass Menagerie,* Production Notes, pp. ix–xii.

I reach for a cigarette, I cross the street, I run into the movies or a bar, I buy a drink, I speak to the nearest stranger—anything that can blow your candles out!

(LAURA *bends over the candles.*)

—for nowadays the world is lit by lightning! Blow out your candles, Laura—and so good-bye. . . .

(*She blows the candles out.*)

THE SCENE DISSOLVES

(Curtain Speech, pp. 123–24)

In *The Glass Menagerie,* then, there is little if any action in the Aristotelian sense; that is, there is in this vision no strict pattern of causal development, from beginning to end. For in the lyric moment, action is aesthetic; it is the growth of understanding. Through his poet-figure, the dramatist invites the spectator to share his fragmentary vision, to re-create his incomplete understanding, and to reflect upon a partial truth about the nature of all human experience. Throughout the fabric of his subsequent work, Williams retains this basic form. At some point in his writing, however, he decided that this drama of "personal lyricism" was too limited an expressive form.[18] The major development of the period immediately following the appearance of *The Glass Menagerie* was the emergence of a second level of dramatic exposition. Above the level of his lyric form, Williams erected an interpretative "scaffold." The plays written after 1945 increasingly show the presence of a kind of superstructure; a rational schema designed to interpret the moment of vision in the language of reason.

18. Preface to *Cat on a Hot Tin Roof,* p. vi.

chapter three

THE SYNTHETIC MYTH

I say that symbols are nothing but the natural speech of drama.

As Tennessee Williams has developed as a dramatist, he has become increasingly concerned about the limitations of a purely lyric form. In the preface to *Cat on a Hot Tin Roof* he records some of his reflections on this problem:

> The fact that I want you to observe what I do for your possible pleasure and to give you knowledge of things that I feel I may know better than you, because my world is different from yours, as different as every man's world is from the world of others, is not enough excuse for a personal lyricism that has not yet mastered its necessary trick of rising above the singular to the plural concern, from personal to general import. But for years and years now, which may have passed like a dream be-

NOTE: The quotation following the chapter title is from the Preface to *Camino Real,* p. x.

cause of this obsession, I have been trying to learn how to perform this trick and make it truthful, and sometimes I feel that I am able to do it. (Preface, pp. vii–viii)

The playwright's problem is indigenous to the expressionistic forms. Indeed, his secondary motive—that of rising from the singular to the plural concern, from expression to meaning—has been voiced by many artists in the past half century. It was articulated as early as 1912 by Wassily Kandinsky and appeared in many of the later treatises published by artists in the Bauhaus School.[1] Some of the concerns voiced by Kandinsky in his early essay, *Concerning the Spiritual in Art,* are recapitulated in Williams' statements:

My own creed as a playwright is fairly close to that expressed by the painter in Shaw's play *The Doctor's Dilemma:* "I believe in Michelangelo, Velasquez and Rembrandt; in the might of design, the mystery of color, the redemption of all things by beauty everlasting and the message of art that has made these hands blessed. Amen."

How much art his hands were blessed with or how much mine are, I don't know, but that art is a blessing is certain and that it contains its message is also certain, and I feel, as the painter did, that the message lies in those abstract beauties of form and color and line, to which I would add light and motion. (Preface to *Camino Real,* pp. xii–xiii)

Williams echoes the interest of the expressionists in an "international state of art." For he suggests that the dramatic form, despite its individuality, must represent more than personal experience, that its contents must be somehow related to the collective consciousness. For Williams the problem of communication in the theatre appears even more critical than comparable difficulties in the plastic arts. For the drama imposes a time limit on understanding. The playwright must articulate his work in such a way that the spectator may grasp its intent within the space of two hours. Moreover, the spectator must believe that his understanding is universal: that his knowledge links him with the whole of humanity, as well as with that particular audience with which he shares a momentary identity.

1. Wassily Kandinsky, *Concerning the Spiritual in Art,* trans. Francis Golffing and others (New York, 1947).

He speaks of this quality of response in the preface (p. x) to *The Rose Tattoo:* "For a couple of hours we may surrender ourselves to a world of fiercely illuminated values in conflict."

Williams recognized early in his career the need for a system of communication, for a theatrical language related specifically to the interpretation of reality in the modern world. The problem has its origin not only in the philosophical position of the dramatist, but also in the vastly extended knowledge of the twentieth century—a knowledge that has proliferated so rapidly it has outrun man's efforts to systematize it. The arts have continued to struggle with the problem of providing a comprehensive linguistic system for the vast accumulation of knowledge which is the legacy of the twentieth century. It is, declares Jean-Paul Sartre, the theatre which must reassume the primary responsibility for defining, ordering, and interpreting truth.[2] Williams' desire to discover universal meaning through drama assumes, in the context of this motive, even greater significance. The attempt to evolve a conventional system of understanding —a catalogue of common meanings—for the drama looms as an undertaking of major importance, not only for this playwright but for the theatre at large.

Francis Fergusson, in his exemplary study *The Idea of a Theater,* traces the drive toward the evolution of a modern theatrical language to Richard Wagner.[3] Wagner attempted to establish for romantic drama a catalogue of symbols through which multiple contents could be given figuration. Fergusson traces Wagner's diagrammatic patterns to many sources: to the Olympian religions, to the iconography of Christianity, and to the imaginative traditions of Northern Europe. Fergusson observes that both the symbolists and the expressionists continued this search for representational systems which could mirror the complex modern consciousness. Some dramatists were successful in discovering such linguistic patterns on native grounds: the plays of Yeats, Synge, O'Casey, and Federico García Lorca are grounded in the poetic pasts of Ireland and Spain. Still other

2. Sartre, "Forgers of Myths," *Theatre Arts,* XXX (June, 1946), 324–35.
3. Fergusson, *The Idea of a Theater* (Princeton, 1949), pp. 80–109.

contemporary dramatists have used the linguistic apparatus of traditional Christian theology: plays such as Paul Claudel's *The Satin Slipper,* T. S. Eliot's *Murder in the Cathedral,* Christopher Fry's *The Boy with a Cart,* and, more recently, Jean Anouilh's *Becket,* Bertolt Brecht's *Galileo,* and John Osborne's *Luther* are partially dependent for their explications upon a language which has its roots in Christian thought and ritual.

The American dramatists have been deeply concerned with the problem of language, especially with the construction of symbolic forms.[4] If Eugene O'Neill's early works such as *Marco Millions* (1923–1925) employed a symbology frankly dependent on European sources, later works such as *Mourning Becomes Electra* (1931) were designed to exploit a pattern of expression which is in larger measure native. As a Southerner, Tennessee Williams has had advantages of consequence: the symbolism of the South, a region separated from the mainstream of the American society by an intricate complex of political, cultural, and economic factors, has greatly enriched the language of the arts. The South, much of which retains many characteristics of primitive societies, has developed in its literature a conventional perspective described by some aestheticians as "Southern agrarianism." Its primordial interpretation of man's struggle in an unfriendly universe has produced a highly developed iconography.

This Southern aesthetic has provided for the drama of Williams a kind of basic linguistic structure comparable to that which appeared in elementary stages of Greek tragedy. For like the Greek myths, this Southern apprehension has a socio-politico-religious grounding in a primitive society where the critical phases of the life struggle are interpreted in an intricate symbolic language.[5] But while Williams employs the Southern

4. See Leon Howard, *Literature and the American Tradition* (New York, 1960), pp. 75–101.

5. This primitive symbology is perhaps most clearly evident in the work of Tennessee Williams. It has, however, been used in certain of O'Neill's works, notably in *The Emperor Jones.* Among the major American dramatists, Thornton Wilder and Arthur Miller seem unaffected by the Southern

symbolism as one element of his syntax, he has attempted, especially in his later works, to progress from this elemental language to a more objective instrument of communication. His "Lord Byron" in *Camino Real* speaks of this process of transliteration:

> But a poet's vocation, which used to be my vocation, is to influence the heart in a gentler fashion than you have made your mark on that loaf of bread. He ought to purify it and lift it above its ordinary level. For what is the heart but a sort of—
>
> [*He makes a high, groping gesture in the air.*]
>
> —A sort of—*instrument!*—that translates *noise* into *music*, *chaos* into —*order* . . . —*a mysterious order!* (Block VIII, p. 77)

As early as *The Glass Menagerie,* Williams began to create myths of modern life; that is, he began to weave the dark images of his personal vision together with certain sociological, psychological, religious, and philosophical contents, in a schematic explication of modern life. This activity, begun in his early work, was accelerated in middle plays such as *A Streetcar Named Desire, Summer and Smoke, Cat on a Hot Tin Roof, The Rose Tattoo,* and *Camino Real.* In these works, the playwright seems to have progressed to the creation of symbols of greater density, richer texture, and more comprehensive philosophical contents than those evident in his earlier plays. Williams comments on his attempt to evolve a more mature theatrical language:

> We all have in our conscious and unconscious minds a great vocabulary of images, and I think all human communication is based on these images as are our dreams; and a symbol in a play has only one legitimate purpose which is to say a thing more directly and simply and beautifully than it could be said in words.
>
> I hate writing that is a parade of images for the sake of images; I hate

"aesthetic." Wilder's *Our Town* is, like O'Neill's *Beyond the Horizon,* a New England play. Miller's *Death of a Salesman,* though set in Brooklyn, seems to reflect a Midwestern mind. It seems to picture a kind of imagination which belongs to the great heartland of America.

it so much that I close a book in disgust when it keeps on saying one thing is like another; I even get disgusted with poems that make nothing but comparisons between one thing and another. But I repeat that symbols, when used respectfully, are the purest language of plays. Sometimes it would take page after tedious page of exposition to put across an idea that can be said with an object or a gesture on the lighted stage.
(Preface to *Camino Real,* pp. x–xi)

Increasingly, the playwright has attempted to create a kind of ideograph in which form and content, feeling and meaning, understanding and reason are wholly unified.[6] Like Brecht, Williams conceives of a symbol so filled with meanings that it embodies the whole of experience within its structural frame. It is clear that one of the major difficulties which the playwright has faced is the need for rational correlatives for personal experience. In *The Glass Menagerie* Williams uses memory as a rationalizing ground, as a point of reference around which his images are clustered. He has obviously found the technique of recall useful; it has enabled him to exercise a high degree of poetic selectivity as well as to defend that distortion which has been necessary to the creation of his symbolic system. The memory device nevertheless has certain disadvantages; it embodies exactly the suggestion of personal limitation which the playwright wishes to transcend. In much of his work, therefore, Williams has employed other devices, many of which are associated with the practices of the surrealists.

In *A Streetcar Named Desire* and in *Summer and Smoke,* Williams creates symbols which have as their rationale progressive insanity. Following André Breton, Salvador Dali, and Giorgio de Chirico, he uses insanity, like intoxication and the dream, as a kind of instrumentation for the organization and interpretation of experience. The insanity mechanism has advantages over the device of memory, especially for works which have tragic implications, for it suggests extremity in human circumstance. The prefrontal lobotomy which threatens Catharine Holly in *Suddenly Last Summer* may thus be read as the

6. Nietzsche describes art as the primary metaphysical activity, because of its function in unifying the "separateness" of life.

equivalent of classical "death." In the same way, the confinement of Blanche to the asylum in *A Streetcar Named Desire* is a sign of annihilation as final in its own way as the murder of Clytemnestra in the *Oresteia.* But the use of the insanity device also presents certain dangers, not only as demonstrated in the work of Williams and others in the contemporary group, but also as seen in the work of traditional dramatists. The question of insanity in *A Streetcar Named Desire* is, in this sense, an extension of a problem affecting earlier plays, including *Orestes, Medea, Hamlet,* and *Miss Julie.* For with the use of insanity as an interpretative instrument, the playwright risks invalidation of his vision. The modern spectator—at least at conscious levels of response—feels himself the moral and intellectual superior of a deranged protagonist. As a linguistic device in contemporary drama, however, insanity is gaining validity. As the horrors of World War II have been exposed, the effect of individual aberration on the course of human affairs has been documented by historical record.

Williams, however, has continued to search for other answers to the problem of objectifying and validating his moments of critical insight. In *Cat on a Hot Tin Roof* he explores the uses of a second scheme. He employs in this play, as in *Sweet Bird of Youth,* another surrealistic device—intoxication. For Brick, truth exists in alcohol: it is alcohol which stops the flow of natural time and freezes the moment of experience in "metaphysical stasis":

BRICK: I have to hear that little click in my head that makes me peaceful. Usually I hear it sooner than this, sometimes as early as—noon, but—

—Today, it's—dilatory. . . .

—I just haven't got the right level of alcohol in my bloodstream yet!

(Act II, pp. 82–83)

Similarly, Alexandra del Lago, the fading movie queen of *Sweet Bird of Youth,* controls her perception of reality—her consciousness—by means of drugs. The decadent "Princess," a priestess in her own right, is the instrument through which the truth is revealed to the spectator as well as to the troubled protagonist Chance.

Williams makes some use of yet a third rationalizing apparatus: the dream organization, a pattern claimed by the surrealists but found throughout the work of Western dramatists. In the prologue to *Camino Real,* the desert rat "Don Quixote" speaks these explanatory lines:

> —And my dream will be a pageant, a masque in which old meanings will be remembered and possibly new ones discovered, and when I wake from this sleep and this disturbing pageant of a dream, I'll choose one among its shadows to take along with me in the place of Sancho. . .
>
> (Prologue, p. 7)

We have noted the dreamlike quality of Williams' visual imagination in the short work *This Property is Condemned.* His setting for *Summer and Smoke* is described in a similar way:

> Now we come to the main exterior set which is a promontory in a park or public square in the town of Glorious Hill. Situated on this promontory is a fountain in the form of a stone angel, in a gracefully crouching position with wings lifted and her hands held together to form a cup from which water flows, a public drinking fountain. The stone angel of the fountain should probably be elevated so that it appears in the background of the interior scenes as a symbolic figure (Eternity) brooding over the course of the play. . . . I would like all three units to form an harmonious whole like one complete picture rather than three separate ones. An imaginative designer may solve these plastic problems in a variety of ways and should not feel bound by any of my specific suggestions.
>
> . . . .
>
> Everything possible should be done to give an unbroken fluid quality to the sequence of scenes.
>
> There should be no curtain except for the intermission. The other divisions of the play should be accomplished by changes of lighting.
>
> Finally, the matter of music. One basic theme should recur and the points of recurrence have been indicated here and there in the stage directions. (Production Notes, pp. ix–x)

In this sequence, then, poetic vision has been released from the restrictions of time, space, and causality. The same dream logic controls poetic vision in *Camino Real.* Williams, in this drama, has effected the kind of montage known to the dreaming mind—the metamorphosis of diverse times, places, and situations into the shape of a single figure, "Camino Real":

> *As the curtain rises, on an almost lightless stage, there is a loud singing of wind, accompanied by distant, measured reverberations like pounding surf, or distant shellfire. Above the ancient wall that backs the set and the perimeter of mountains visible above the wall, are flickers of a white radiance as though daybreak were a white bird caught in a net and struggling to rise.*
>
> *The plaza is seen fitfully by this light. It belongs to a tropical seaport that bears a confusing, but somehow harmonious, resemblance to such widely scattered ports as Tangiers, Havana, Vera Cruz, Casablanca, Shanghai, New Orleans.* (Prologue, p. 1)

But if Williams is indebted to the surrealists for much of his language, he also employs in his work another kind of symbolic apparatus which may be traced to the scientific thinkers of the late nineteenth century. In *Cat on a Hot Tin Roof* he develops a kind of symbolism which is indebted to the great scientific naturalists, especially to Herbert Spencer and Charles Darwin. Williams interprets human existence as life in a great "zoo," a retrogressive step from the "glass menagerie." Big Daddy Pollitt describes humanity (Act II, p. 72) in these naturalistic terms: "The human animal is a beast that dies but the fact that he's dying don't give him pity for others, no sir. . . ." In this work, Williams describes human existence in "biological" nomenclature. As he follows the example of the naturalists in positing biological existence as the fundamental "ground of reality," he is able to equate the loss of the procreative power as a sign of death. Similarly, he reveals the fate of Big Daddy Pollitt by showing his fearful deterioration as the victim of a corrosive disease.

This naturalistic symbolism permits Williams to conduct several kinds of explorations simultaneously. In *Cat on a Hot Tin Roof* he examines a social condition, reveals the inner life of the individuals who are affected, and shows the larger implications of the naturalist philosophy in the interpretation of the moral universe. The sickness of Brick therefore becomes the pivot for the penetration of an entire fabric of moral problems. Williams describes the protagonist's dilemma in this way:

> *The thing they're discussing, timidly and painfully on the side of Big Daddy, fiercely, violently on Brick's side, is the inadmissible thing that Skipper died to disavow between them. The fact that if it existed it had to be disavowed to "keep face" in the world they lived in, may be at the heart of the "mendacity" that Brick drinks to kill his disgust with. It may be the root of his collapse. Or maybe it is only a single manifestation of it, not even the most important. The bird that I hope to catch in the net of this play is not the solution of one man's psychological problem. I am trying to catch the true quality of experience in a group of people, that cloudy, flickering, evanescent—fiercely charged!—interplay of live human beings in the thundercloud of a common crisis. Some mystery should be left in the revelation of character in a play, just as a great deal of mystery is always left in the revelation of character in life, even in one's own character to himself. This does not absolve the playwright of his duty to observe and probe as clearly and deeply as he* legitimately *can: but it should steer him away from "pat" conclusions, facile definitions which make a play just a play, not a snare for the truth of human experience.* (Act II, pp. 98–99)

With the aid of his biological symbology, Williams reconsiders a theme drawn from Greek tragedy. *Cat on a Hot Tin Roof* is a study of an extended cycle of human transgression. As Big Daddy Pollitt perceives the working out of the curse upon his house, he cries out, in Aeschylean tones, his malediction:

> CHRIST—DAMN—ALL—LYING SONS OF—LYING BITCHES!
>
> . . . .
>
> Yes, all liars, all liars, all lying dying liars!
>
> . . . .
>
> —Lying! Dying! Liars! (Act II, p. 112)

Of all Williams' plays, *Cat on a Hot Tin Roof* seems to have a movement most nearly like that of Greek drama. Its progression is, in many ways, tragic in kind. Williams indicates that he was conscious of this parallelism. The playwright suggests, however, that he was persuaded by the director to arrest the forward movement of the drama's tragic descent and to substitute for it a modified denouement. He describes the rationale which dictated this change:

No living playwright, that I can think of, hasn't something valuable to learn about his own work from a director so keenly perceptive as Elia Kazan. It so happened that in the case of *Streetcar,* Kazan was given a script that was completely finished. In the case of *Cat,* he was shown the first typed version of the play, and he was excited by it, but he had definite reservations about it which were concentrated in the third act. The gist of his reservations can be listed as three points: one, he felt that Big Daddy was too vivid and important a character to disappear from the play except as an offstage cry after the second act curtain; two, he felt that the character of Brick should undergo some apparent mutation as a result of the virtual vivisection that he undergoes in his interview with his father in Act Two. Three, he felt that the character of Margaret, while he understood that I sympathized with her and liked her myself, should be, if possible, more clearly sympathetic to an audience.

It was only the third of these suggestions that I embraced wholeheartedly from the outset, because it so happened that Maggie the Cat had become steadily more charming to me as I worked on her characterization. I didn't want Big Daddy to reappear in Act Three and I felt that the moral paralysis of Brick was a root thing in his tragedy, and to show a dramatic progression would obscure the meaning of that tragedy in him and because I don't believe that a conversation, however revelatory, ever effects so immediate a change in the heart or even conduct of a person in Brick's state of spiritual disrepair.

However, I wanted Kazan to direct the play, and though these suggestions were not made in the form of an ultimatum, I was fearful that I would lose his interest if I didn't re-examine the script from his point of view. I did.[7]

The change here is more than an alteration in stage directions. Insofar as this discussion is concerned, it represents a major adjustment in the cycle of action, an adjustment which moved the drama from its original position as a near-tragedy to a point in proximity to the thesis play of realist definition. For in terms of the symbolism to which Williams had committed

7. Playwright's "Note of Explanation" on alternative ending to Act III, *Cat on a Hot Tin Roof,* pp. 151–52.

himself in the early moments of the drama, there could have developed only complete and final catastrophe for the House of Pollitt.

Gradually, in his later works, Williams has put together a kind of modern myth, a symbolic representation of the life of man in our time. His myth is not an organic form; that is, it is not a fabric surfacing from the unconscious life of man, individual or collective. In this sense it differs from the great natural structures which have evolved through world religions and even from popular myths, such as those which now surround the figure of the legendary American cowboy. The contemporary myth of Williams is synthetic. It is composed, after the manner of cinematic montage, from the fragments of many ethical, philosophic, social, poetic, intellectual, and religious perspectives. But this synthetic structure must in this respect be accounted valid; for it is the image of modern man caught between opposing logics—man in search of a means of reconciliation. The myth of Williams mirrors modern man's dilemma—his need for a comprehensive system of interpretation, for a structure which can restore meaning to life and which can reconcile the conflict within reality itself.

In a seminar on *Camino Real* convened at Bochum, Germany, in 1953, some of the latent contents in Williams' myth were discussed at length.[8] The scholars on that occasion identified his linguistic structure as expressionist in kind, but pointed out that his form has been clothed in symbolic contents which are specifically related to the "American imagination." They noted that Williams the observer, standing at mid-point in the twentieth century, has attempted in his work to represent all the forces, ideas, values, systems of thought, and modes of behavior which impinge upon the position of the American in

8. Transcription of the Bochum Festival, *Bochumer Diskussion über "Camino Real" von Tennessee Williams* (Frankfurt-am-Main, 1955), pp. 5–14. The English translation used here is that of Gerald Gillespie.

our time. There appear to be three major schemata which provide a scaffold for this synthetic structure: the ritual myth of the theatre, the literary myth of the twentieth-century American, and the Freudian-Jungian myth of modern man.

Williams attempts to interpret vision with the help of an apparatus described by Fergusson as the *myth of the theatre.*[9] It was Nietzsche who rationalized Shakespeare's perception of the "world as theatre," the "theatre as world." Many contemporaries, including the existentialists, have pursued this line of reasoning and have suggested that the theatre is the ground of ultimate reality, the instrument for discovering permanent truths. Williams employs this apprehension throughout his work. In *The Glass Menagerie* the protagonist articulates a proposition which reverses the normal order of reality by positing the stage as the ground of ultimate truth.

Throughout all of his work, Williams follows a plan which theatricalizes—even ritualizes—ordinary experience. Consider this description from the short sketch, *The Unsatisfactory Supper or The Long Stay Cut Short:*

> THE CURTAIN RISES *on the porch and side yard of a shotgun cottage in Blue Mountain, Mississippi. The frame house is faded and has a greenish-gray cast with dark streaks from the roof, and there are irregularities in the lines of the building. Behind it the dusky cyclorama is stained with the rose of sunset, which is stormy-looking, and the wind has a cat-like whine.*
>
> *Upstage from the porch, in the center of the side yard, is a very large rose-bush, the beauty of which is somehow sinister-looking.*
>
> *A Prokofief sort of music introduces the scene and sets a mood of grotesque lyricism.*
>
> *The screen door opens with a snarl of rusty springs and latches: this stops the music.*
>
> . . . .
>
> *(The evenly cadenced lines of the dialogue between* BABY DOLL *and* ARCHIE LEE *may be given a singsong reading, somewhat like a grotesque choral incantation, and passages may be divided as strophe and antistrophe by* BABY DOLL'S *movements back and forth on the porch.)*
>
> (In *American Blues,* pp. 33–34)

9. Fergusson, *The Idea of a Theater,* pp. 206–40.

There is a similar ritualization of action in *Cat on a Hot Tin Roof*. The playwright's instructions for Maggie's opening soliloquy give some indication of this anti-realist approach:

In her long speeches she has the vocal tricks of a priest delivering a liturgical chant, the lines are almost sung, always continuing a little beyond her breath. . . .

In this drama, Williams has scored his record of suffering with the primitive incantations of children and servants:

Skinamarinka–dinka–dink
Skinamarinka—do
We love you.
Skinamarinka—dinka–dink
Skinamarinka—do. (Act II, p. 52)

Williams attempts to recover to the theatre a primary article of faith, the primitive belief in the magical power of mime. In this and other works, he attempts to release his theatre from realist restrictions and to reintroduce into the drama aspects of its original incantatory identity.

While Williams' symbols are to some degree indebted to the religious legends of the ancient Greeks and of the Northern Europeans, there are, woven into his myth of the theatre, many figures drawn from Christian ritual. For Williams, like Shakespeare, is haunted with images of the suffering Christ. His works abound with symbols drawn from the passion plays: the *Redemption of Mary Magdalene; Christ before Pilate;* the *Crucifixion;* the *Descent from the Cross;* the *Harrowing of Hell;* and the *Sorrowing Mother of God*. Some of these figures may be seen in the verse play, *The Purification*. Here Williams ritualizes a description of the murder of the girl Elena:

RANCHER: Yes.
I set up the ladder.
SON: Set up the steep, steep ladder—
Narrow . . .
RANCHER: Narrow!—Enquiring
If Christ be still on the Cross!
CHORUS: Cross!
SON: Against the north wall set it . . .

RANCHER: Set it and climbed . . .
(*He clutches his forehead*). Climbed!
CHORUS: Climbed!
SON: Climbed!
To the side of the loft
that gave all things to the sky.
The axe—
for a single moment—
saluted the moon—then struck!
CHORUS: Struck!
SON: And she didn't cry . . .
RANCHER: Struck!
Aye, struck, struck, struck!
CHORUS: Struck!

(Dissonant chords on the guitar, with cymbals. The two men surge together and struggle like animals till they are torn apart. There is a rumble of thunder.) (In *27 Wagons Full of Cotton,* pp. 48–49)

Another variation on the "crucifixion" theme appears in the final scene of *Orpheus Descending,* where the protagonist is incinerated with an acetylene torch:

VOICES OF MEN [*shouting*]:—Keep to the walls!
He's armed!
—Upstairs, Dog!
—Jack, the confectionery!
[*Wild cry back of store.*]
Got him, GOT HIM!
—Rope, git rope!
—Git rope from th' hardware section!
—I got something better than rope!
—What've you got?
—What's that, what's he got?
—A BLOWTORCH!
—Christ . . . (Act III, Scene 3, p. 116)

But Williams' exploitation of Christian mythology is more comprehensive than this use of symbolic motif. The Christian interpretation of the life cycle is played over and over again in his drama. In his early works, Williams' version of the Christian cycle is truncated. In *The Glass Menagerie,* the playwright stops the movement of his progression of suffering and announces that the play, as yet without a philosophical resolution, is over. The poet, in this early work, persuades the spectator to accept an aesthetic conclusion: the creation of the drama itself. In *A Streetcar Named Desire,* the cycle of suffering does not progress to the point of clear resolution; Blanche "dies," and we are merely promised a new life in Stella's unborn child. In certain of the later works, however, the spiritual renewal of the protagonist is completed. The gradual change reflected in Brick, like the enlightenment of the priest Shannon in *The Night of the Iguana,* seems, however, to represent a resolution which is primarily Christian rather than Greek in nature. Like Shakespeare in *The Winter's Tale,* Williams attempts to transcend the tragic effect of human action by superimposing an essentially Christian resolution. Like Leontes, his protagonist is redeemed by the power of human compassion.

Intimately related to his apprehension of human action is the playwright's image of character. For Williams, man is the great sinner, the transgressor against moral law. In his explication of the dilemma of modern man, Williams is partially dependent on a fundamental and unsophisticated theology. Like St. Paul, he views human existence as a condition necessarily marked by unavoidable transgression. He draws man as a creature in need of a mode of salvation, in search of a power which can transcend that vested in natural life. Like many orthodox Christian theologians, Williams defines this saving power as human love. It is not surprising that there appears throughout the fabric of his work much of the linguistic apparatus of Christian theology: especially its progression of sin, suffering, guilt, punishment, and expiation. Moreover, Williams prescribes a theological resolution for human suffering. He superimposes on his dark cycle of suffering a transcendent progression of love, sympathy, contrition, sacrifice, and understanding.

Through his rite of the theatre, then, Williams plays out modern man's search for salvation. If he interprets the condition of man through this fundamental symbology, he also employs more sophisticated perceptions. Through his myth of the twentieth-century American, he attempts to relate many individually-oriented perceptions to the larger question of the destiny of civilization. Williams is especially concerned with the illumination of the role of the American in the world of the twentieth century. For this purpose he has had recourse to a technique employed by James Joyce, Ezra Pound, and T. S. Eliot. He has composed a "myth of human development" in which the milestones in man's progress—or retrogression—are marked by literary achievement.

Williams attempts to interpret the complex historical role of "the American" on the contemporary world stage. In each of his plays he describes a region of this native ground: St. Louis, New Orleans, the Delta, Glorious Hill, Mississippi, and an assortment of Central American towns. It is important to recognize that Williams' geography is essentially imaginative: the region of conflict which he symbolizes is the modern American mind. Beneath the personal accounts which form the bases of his dramas, there rages a critical struggle between ways of life. In *A Streetcar Named Desire* he polarizes this conflict in the school teacher Blanche, with her talk of poetry and arts, and the laborer Kowalski, with his life of animal joys. Blanche describes her antagonist in these terms:

> He acts like an animal, has an animal's habits! Eats like one, moves like one, talks like one! There's even something—sub-human—something not quite to the stage of humanity yet! Yes, something—ape-like about him, like one of those pictures I've seen in—anthropological studies! Thousands and thousands of years have passed him right by, and there he is—Stanley Kowalski—survivor of the stone age! Bearing the raw meat home from the kill in the jungle! . . . Maybe we are a long way from being made in God's image, but Stella—my sister—there has been *some* progress since then! Such things as art—as poetry and music—such kinds of new light have come into the world since then! In some kinds of people some tenderer feelings have had some little beginning! That we have got to make *grow!* And *cling* to, and hold as our flag! In this dark march to whatever it is we're approaching . . . . *Don't—don't hang back with the brutes!* (Scene IV, pp. 80–81)

In *Summer and Smoke* the playwright continues his exploration of a major societal conflict. In this play, the protagonist Alma is described (Scene I, p. 15) as a symbol of traditional humanist values: "She seems to belong to a more elegant age, such as the Eighteenth Century in France." It is in fact her disorientation from the contemporary world of Glorious Hill, Mississippi, which is the cause of Alma's destruction. In the end, it is the animalistic John Buchanan who—like Stanley Kowalski—conquers this representative of past civilizations. In certain later plays, Williams attributes successful conquest to his women. It is Maggie, for example, who lives and wins by the law of nature, as it is Alexandra del Lago in *Sweet Bird of Youth* and the widow Faulk in *The Night of the Iguana* who hold aloft the flag of the jungle. Through these representative characters, Williams explores the question of choice for civilization itself, a choice between past and present, between soul and body. If the myth of the theatre interprets individual destiny in the moral universe, the myth of the American attempts to relate individual morality to societal conflict.

Perhaps the most familiar formation within Williams' linguistic structure is one that may be described as his *psychological myth.* So important has this structure been to the explication of the playwright's vision that it has often been interpreted as a primary element of his content. Although the boundary between form and content is exceedingly difficult to determine, it is an especially important distinction in the interpretation of Williams' work. For in the drama of Williams, the psychological myth is primarily linguistic in nature; that is to say, it attempts to determine how, not why, life occurs. Williams' psychological myth may be traced to many sources. While its immediate indebtedness to the researches of Freud is apparent, it illustrates clearly the dependence of Freudian theory on perceptions out of the Greek and Judaeo-Christian traditions. Indeed, many of the Christian apprehensions which the playwright employs find parallels in the schemata of Freud. For example, the triadic concept of reality associated with Christian theology has its counterpart in Freud's organization of the ego, super-ego, and id. Moreover, Freud provides objective equivalents for the same phenomena which are given signification in the Christian cycle of sin-guilt-expiation–catharsis. Both Christian mythology and the Freudian system—like certain Greek apprehensions of the Olympian, Homeric, and Hellenic periods—appear to be concerned with the same psychic phenomena.

Williams benefits from this pattern of correspondences in human apprehension and is able to exploit it in the construct of his own myth. For he uses the Freudian language as a system for designating reality, its tripartite divisions as signs of modes of experience, and its clinical nomenclature as a description of universal human distress. David Sievers, in his study *Freud on Broadway,* gives this explanation to Williams' use of sexual psychology in *A Streetcar Named Desire:* "Williams arranges in compelling theatrical pattern the agonized sexual anxiety of a girl caught between *id* and *ego-ideal."* [10] Sievers is correct in his analysis; however, sexual anxiety in the theatre of Williams is a symptom of a more comprehensive form of despair. Its meaning is grounded in the relationship of both Williams and Freud to larger patterns in intellectual history. Williams, like Freud, establishes human personality in its animal origins. For both, sexuality is the symbol of being. While later thinkers in the psychological disciplines have tended to modify the rigid system of early Freudian psychology, artists such as Williams have retained much of this older language, primarily because it is easier to project than the more abstract concepts such as social acceptance, the will-to-power, or the will-to-meaning. Williams has taken his point of departure from a primitive interpretation of sexual anxiety as life anxiety. From this point of view, it is possible to suggest that the dramatist, in all of his work, is concerned with the same range of

10. W. David Sievers, *Freud on Brodway* (New York, 1955), p. 377.

human problems that engage a large group of contemporary thinkers and artists.

Williams looks at man's inner life through his Freudian "glass," an interpretative apparatus which has particular meaning in the tradition of American letters. One of the most striking examples of his poetic use of this language may be seen in his explication of crisis in *Cat on a Hot Tin Roof*. This drama seeks to examine the condition of modern man through certain perceptions associated with the naturalist philosophies of Darwin, Spencer, Marx, and others. Such perceptions show man as an animal struggling for supremacy, displaying the superiority of his will-to-live in a jungle filled with other animals. But Williams also explores in this work the devastating effect of unqualified acceptance of the naturalist ontologies. He projects above his primary and secondary images yet a third image: a picture of humanity characterized by growing despair, by the "sickness unto death." When Europeans such as Jean-Paul Sartre treat similar themes, they tend to define them in philosophical, even ideological, terms. Such is the mode of treatment which Sartre accords his *Prisoners at Altona,* a portrayal of a family that has marked similarities to Williams' House of Pollitt. But while Sartre explains the decay of the German industrialist and his scions in philosophical and neopolitical terms, Williams describes the "Fall of the House of Big Daddy Pollitt" in the language of Freud.

In *Cat on a Hot Tin Roof,* then, sexual failures are but the outer sign of inner disaster. For the true themes of the drama are metaphysical loneliness, nausea, and despair. Williams describes these stages in the existential progression in clinical language. He connotes Brick's loneliness—his alienation from friend, wife, father, mother, and God—through a series of clinically described symptoms. He describes his nausea through his lack of interest in all human relations. He defines his dread in a classically composed pattern of vacillation, from impotence to overcompensation. Williams interprets the crisis in this play as Brick's failure to understand the nature of his own existence —a failure which the playwright describes as "latent homosexuality." Despite the nature of the communicative structure employed, the main theme of the play is not sexual anxiety. *Cat on a Hot Tin Roof,* according to Williams' own definition, is a study of "mendacity," an image of falsity in life. Williams' protagonist suffers from "the sickness unto death," from that despair born of transgression, guilt, and alienation.

The British critic E. Martin Browne comments on this play in the preface to an English edition:

> To an Englishman, he opens a vision of the size of America, the huge fertility which can place apparently inexhaustible power in a man's hands . . . "twenty-eight thousand acres of the richest land this side of the valley Nile." Big Daddy is a patriarch: he reminds one of a character in Genesis (perhaps from the less frequently quoted chapters); he has the same warmth of the soil in him. The best poetry of the play is in his speeches, which distil the wisdom of primitive human nature.
>
> Brick and his Cat, the centres of the drama, vibrate in their desperation with the heat of the South. The family is clothed with the atmosphere of the South as with a garment. It is caged in the hot, thin-walled house, a prison amid the vast, rich lands around it. Tennessee Williams' use of repetition to create a prison of words is extraordinarily skilful: words beat like a tattoo on the heart, yet the beat is subtly changed at each hearing. This evocative quality of rhythm again reminds one of Synge. Perhaps it is no accident that in both writers the quality springs from a sad soil . . . .
>
> American drama, as it comes to maturity, enlarges the horizons of the theatre.[11]

Williams approximates, in this modern myth, the Greek horror of crime against life. Brick, like Oedipus the King, is a man guilty of a crime, a transgression so dread that neither he nor his family dare to speak its name. Williams finds in homosexuality an equivalent for the Greek sin of incest. Through this parallel, he is able to illumine a pattern of correspondences between that archaic civilization and our own.

A close study of Williams' use of psychology shows that the playwright has modified the rigid structure of the early Freudian system with other related perspectives, the most im-

11. Preface to *Cat on a Hot Tin Roof* (London, 1956), p. 5.

portant of which is the poetic construct of Carl Gustav Jung. For Williams, Jung's theories meet certain problems for which the Freudian orthodoxy does not provide explication. The most obvious of these necessary arrangements is Jung's theory of image-making: his concept of primordial and archaic forms written in the collective unconscious. This theory, basically that cited by Williams in his own discussion of image-making, has been extremely useful to a large group of contemporary artists who have required a way of rationalizing their own perceptions.

Perhaps the chief value of Jung to Williams and others is the kind of poetic ambiguity embodied in his theory of images. Jung wrote in a discussion of poetic types,

> The great problems of life . . . are always related to the primordial images of the collective unconscious. These images are really balancing or compensating factors which correspond with the problems life presents in actuality.
>
> This is not to be marvelled at, since these images are deposits, representing the accumulated experience of thousands of years of struggle for adaptation and existence. Every great experience in life, every profound conflict, evokes the treasured wealth of these images and brings them to inner perception; as such, they become accessible to consciousness only in the presence of that degree of self-awareness and power of understanding which enables a man to think what he experiences instead of just living it blindly. In the latter case he actually lives the myth and the symbol without knowing it.[12]

Unlike Freud, Jung considers, in his system, all aspects of human experience, even those phenomena for which he can offer no scientific explanation:

> I can only gaze with wonder and awe at the depths and heights of our psychic nature. Its non-spatial nature conceals an untold abundance of images which have accumulated over millions of years of living development and become fixed in the organism. My consciousness is like an eye that penetrates to the most distant places, yet it is the psychic non-ego that fills them with non-spatial images. And these images are not pale shadows, but tremendously powerful psychic factors. The most we may

12. Carl Gustav Jung, *Psychological Types,* trans. H. Godwin Baynes (London, 1923), pp. 271–72.

be able to do is misunderstand them, but we can never rob them of their power by denying them.[13]

Jung's system is a more flexible and indeed a more poetically conceived schema than that of the scientist Freud. While Jung has attempted in his work to systematize human experience and to submit human personality to scientific scrutiny, his psychology retains a poetic ambiguity—a recognition of the impenetrability of those aspects of experience which Wagner described as "unknowable." His theory of the collective unconscious, with its roots in racial memory, provides therefore an epistemology consistent with the poetic interests of Williams.

A second advantage for Williams lies in Jung's eclecticism, in his ability to synthesize a large group of perceptions relevant to the life of Western man. In his theory of archetypes, Jung provides a symbolic structure that is concerned with the meaning of the whole pattern of Western history: cultural, political, social, and intellectual.[14] Williams finds an appropriately poetic symbol for human experience in Jung's concept of the "human odyssey," the journey toward understanding.[15] But while Jungian psychology takes account of a universe in conflict—the broken world of Williams' description—its essentially aesthetic view of experience provides hope of individual reconciliation. If Williams borrows from Freud his apparatus for the description of suffering humanity, he gains from the construct of Jung justification for his hope of salvation. For Jung, like Williams, offers art as the chief instrument of human reconciliation:

Nobody can stand the total loss of the archetype. When that happens, it gives rise to that "frightful discontent in our culture," where nobody feels at home because a "father" and "mother" are missing. Everyone

13. Jung, *Freud and Psychoanalysis,* in *Collected Works,* eds. Herbert Read, Michael Fordham, and Gerhard Adler, trans. R. F. C. Hull (New York and London, 1953–6?), IV, 332.

14. See Ira Progoff, *Jung's Psychology and Its Social Meaning* (New York, 1953), p. 13.

15. See Jung, *Modern Man in Search of a Soul* (New York, 1934).

knows the provisions that religion has always made in this respect. Unfortunately there are very many people who thoughtlessly go on asking whether these provisions are "true," when it is really a question of a psychological need. Nothing is achieved by explaining them away rationalistically.[16]

Jung confirms Williams' belief that the great conflicts of life are made whole as images:

> Eternal truth needs a human language that alters with the spirit of the times. The primordial images undergo ceaseless transformation and yet remain ever the same, but only in a new form can they be understood anew. Always they require a new interpretation if, as each formulation becomes obsolete, they are not to lose their spellbinding power. . . . Where are the answers to the spiritual needs and troubles of a new epoch? And where the knowledge to deal with the psychological problems raised by the development of modern consciousness? Never before has "eternal" truth been faced with such a hybris of will and power.[17]

In Jung's poetic image of the odyssey—the journey toward meaning, the search for self and soul—Williams finds a symbol for the reality of his description. Moreover, he finds in Jungian theory justification for his belief in art as a mode of transcendence, as a reconciling symbol in which the conflicts of life may be effectively resolved.

It is, then, this synthetic myth—a structure consciously composed from diverse moral, intellectual, social, political, and symbolic perspectives—which is one of the major characteristics of the theatre of Tennessee Williams. Although European dramatists have themselves devised such an eclectic construct, they have used, in the main, philosophical, literary, and ideological perceptions as the raw materials of their myths. Jean-Paul Sartre has written that French dramatists have eschewed biological and psychological explications of reality because of their grounding in the limited apprehensions of the nineteenth-century naturalists. Americans have, on the contrary, employed

16. "Concerning the Archetypes," from *The Archetypes and the Collective Unconscious,* in *Collected Works,* IX, Part I, 69.

17. Jung, "Psychology of Transference," from *The Practice of Psychotherapy,* in *Collected Works,* XVI, 195–96.

perceptions which reflect the bias of a somewhat different heritage.

As Williams has succeeded in familiarizing his audiences—and his interpreters—with his conventional system of explication, many of the latent meanings of his work have come into view. Despite the effectiveness of his myth, the drama of Williams has retained, nonetheless, a fundamental inner division: an antagonism between feeling and reason, expression and meaning. For the process of synthesis has not yet been completed. Although Williams has gained from many sources—including the structures of Carl Gustav Jung—support for his system-building, his work has not yet overcome the fundamental problem of the modern arts: the evolution of a truly effective mode of aesthetic transcendence. There remains within the structural form—if not in the vision itself—an inorganicism, a critical tension between motion and arrest, the concrete and the abstract, experience and art.

chapter four

THE ANTI-HERO

Caught in the form of limitation
Between un-being and being.

One of the most controversial aspects of the drama of Tennessee Williams is his use of an anti-heroic protagonist as an image of man. Williams appears to reject the Aristotelian concept of the protagonist and to substitute for it an anti-hero, the personification of a humanity neither good, knowledgeable, nor courageous. In Blanche, Alma, Brick, Kilroy, Val, Chance, and Shannon, we see this anti-heroic image of man. Even those figures who command some sympathy, characters such as Tom in *The Glass Menagerie* and Catharine—the victim of *Suddenly*

NOTE: The quotation following the chapter title is from a poem by T. S. Eliot, "Burnt Norton," which appears in *Four Quartets* (London: Faber and Faber, 1949), p. 20; copyright 1943, by Harcourt, Brace & World, Inc., and reprinted with their permission.

Last Summer—may be described in the language of T. S. Eliot as "non-beings"—"Caught in the form of limitation/Between un-being and being." Williams claims that such is the image of modern man—poised as he is between the contrary imperatives of his world. As he examines humanity through the patched glass of his synthetic myth, the playwright perceives a creature transfixed in a moment of stasis, halted at the point of transition in the process of becoming.[1]

In the "East Coker" movement of *Four Quartets,* T. S. Eliot describes the moral universe out of which the anti-hero has emerged:

> . . . There is, it seems to us,
> At best, only a limited value
> In the knowledge derived from experience.
> The knowledge imposes a pattern, and falsifies,
> For the pattern is new in every moment
> And every moment is a new and shocking
> Valuation of all we have been. We are only undeceived
> Of that which, deceiving, could no longer harm.
> In the middle, not only in the middle of the way
> But all the way, in a dark wood, in a bramble,
> On the edge of a grimpen, where is no secure foothold,
> And menaced by monsters, fancy lights,
> Risking enchantment. Do not let me hear
> Of the wisdom of old men, but rather of their folly,
> Their fear of fear and frenzy, their fear of possession,
> Of belonging to another, or to others, or to God.
> The only wisdom we can hope to acquire
> Is the wisdom of humility: humility is endless.[2]

Williams throughout his work—fictional, poetic, and dramatic—portrays the humanity mirrored in Eliot's lines. He attempts to show us man "On the edge of a grimpen, where

1. Williams, like Eliot and others among twentieth-century artists, accepts a dynamic theory of reality. Like post-Hegelians such as Bergson, Williams regards art as the image of process, and form as a "still" picture drawn out of the moving spectacle. See Henri Bergson, *An Introduction to Metaphysics,* trans. T. E. Hulme (New York: The Liberal Arts Press, 1949), pp. 25–27.

2. "East Coker" in *Four Quartets* (London: Faber and Faber, 1949), pp. 26–27; copyright 1943, by Harcourt, Brace & World, Inc., and reprinted with their permission.

is no secure foothold,/And menaced by monsters, fancy lights,/ Risking enchantment." The reasons for these adjustments in the image of man are clear. The definition of the hero given in the *Poetics* of Aristotle does not adapt itself to the contemporary perception of reality. For Aristotle, like Plato, conceived virtues to be relatively static concepts.[3] His hero is the personification of "good," a man possessing a significant distribution of those qualities which the philosopher believed to characterize the highest levels of human life. Aristotle thought moral stability, like intelligence, to be the concomitant of aristocratic birth. His definition of character thus reflects the political, social, ethical, and religious biases of his own age: "There remains, then, the character between these two extremes,—that of a man who is not eminently good and just, yet whose misfortune is brought about not by vice or depravity, but by some error or frailty."[4]

Although contemporary dramatists accept certain aspects of the ethics of Aristotle, they do not feel that his definition of the hero is in every sense an accurate description of a virtuous man in the twentieth century. Arthur Miller, for example, points out that many aspects of Aristotle's system of ethics are today obsolete. The image of man in the twentieth century, writes Miller, must be rooted in an open system of values appropriate to a democratic society.[5] Tennessee Williams writes that the most pressing moral problem of man in the twentieth century is to avoid extinction: "to beat the game of being against non-being."[6] The crux of the argument which has led to the modification of the Aristotelian hero lies in changes in the perception of experience, in the accumulation of new knowledges about and new hopes for the human species.

One of the most dramatic of the changes which have affected the idea of the hero is that embodied in the science of psychol-

3. See also Aristotle *Ethics,* trans. D. P. Chase (London, 1911).

4. Butcher, *Aristotle's Theory of Poetry* . . . (New York, 1951), p 45.

5. Arthur Miller, Introduction to the *Collected Plays* (New York, 1957), pp. 8–12.

6. Introduction to *The Rose Tattoo,* p. ix.

ogy, for classic ideals of "goodness," "nobility," and "courage" have, under psychological scrutiny, assumed a significantly different aspect. Equally affecting, perhaps, has been the political history of modern Europe: a record of suffering, wars, and conflicts which have exacted a tremendous physical, spiritual, and psychological toll. Because of a new sense of historical crisis, the hero, a man of action, has grown less appealing as an image of present moral and ethical aspirations than the anti-hero, a man of reflection and contemplation. But perhaps an even more profound change in perspective is represented in the growing influence of the Judaeo-Christian ethic on the moral aspirations of the common man. Despite the apparent record of history, the principles of Christianity have become, in the past century, a more meaningful part of a common standard for human action. The substitution of the "inner-oriented" ethic of the Christian protagonist for the "outer-directed" heroism of the Greek hero is one of the significant contemporary adjustments in Western drama. It is this change which has materially altered the idea of tragic action and which has produced a new concept of dramatic character.[7]

In a discussion of contemporary form, René-Marill Albérès describes the contemporary anti-hero as a "theological protagonist." He is an image of man seeking to know the universe, to define its purpose, and to discover his ultimate meaning in its pattern. Albérès describes the contemporary motive in these words: "The contemporary theatre, like the novel, becomes a research and a quest. It makes itself idealistic, its characters force themselves toward that which they can never find." [8] For Albérès the anti-heroic quest is a journey toward moral commitment. Williams seems to confirm this judgment in his play

7. Such a change in perspective appears in late Greek drama, especially in plays such as *Oedipus at Colonus,* a work which shows many correspondences to "Christian drama." In the main, however, the movement toward an "inner direction" must be attributed to the passage of Christian perspectives into the medieval drama.

8. René-Marill Albérès, *La Révolte des écrivains d'aujourd'hui* (Paris, 1949), p. 141. (The translation is my own.)

The Night of the Iguana; he gives in this work the account of a heretic, the story of the world-weary priest Shannon who searches the earth for the face of God. Shannon follows the moral progression described by St. John of the Cross as the "dark night of the soul." He proceeds in contrary motion, in flight from the presence of God; but, like St. John, he finds that the "way down" leads up. Shannon declares that his search has brought him finally to that presence which he has sought:

> Yes, I see him, I hear him, I know him. And if he doesn't know that I know him, let him strike me dead with a bolt of his lightning.
>
> (Act II, p. 78)

Williams' construction of his anti-heroic protagonist, his "negative saint," is based on a radical perception of new dangers for mankind, as well as on the recognition of new modes of courage. What are these dangers? In *A Streetcar Named Desire* the playwright cautions the spectator against societal regression, against the capitulation of humanity to the laws of the jungle. In later plays—*Cat on a Hot Tin Roof, Camino Real, Suddenly Last Summer, Sweet Bird of Youth,* and *The Night of the Iguana*—he warns against the moral and spiritual disintegration of mankind. To interpret present dimensions of the human dilemma, Williams creates a protagonist who is conceived in anti-traditional terms. Brick, Kilroy, Catharine, Chance, and Shannon are not "mankind" in the sense of classic, neoclassic, romantic, or realistic definitions. They are images of a humanity diminished by time and history. They are each characterized by an inner division, by a fragmentation so complete that it has reduced them to partialities. They are "un-beings," caught in the destructive life-process. They are fragments of debris, thrown up by "time the destroyer."[9] In the short story *One Arm,* Williams describes this anti-heroic man: "He never said to himself, I'm lost. But the speechless self knew it and in

9. This is Eliot's phrase. It appears in "The Dry Salvages," the third of *The Four Quartets* (London: Faber and Faber, 1949): "Time the destroyer is time the preserver," p. 40, line 115; copyright 1943, by Harcourt, Brace & World, Inc., and reprinted with their permission.

submission to its unthinking control the youth had begun as soon as he left the hospital to look about for destruction."[10]

The portrait of the anti-hero is not confined to the work of this playwright. Its fusion of pessimism and mysticism was the trademark of both the poetic realists and the early expressionists. The image of an anti-heroic man may be seen in the plays of Strindberg, Tolstoy, Ibsen, and Chekhov, as well as in the writings of expressionist artists such as Oskar Kokoschka. Moreover, this same contour is apparent in the work of existential dramatists such as Jean-Paul Sartre and Albert Camus. Some of the most telling portraits of the anti-hero have appeared in the work of the orthodox Christian dramatists Paul Claudel and T. S. Eliot. Claudel's *Partage de Midi,* like Eliot's *Murder in the Cathedral,* interprets an anti-heroic image with eloquence. Eliot gives the human condition anti-heroic description in these lines:

> Man's life is a cheat and a disappointment;
> All things are unreal,
> Unreal or disappointing:
> The Catherine wheel, the pantomime cat,
> The prizes given at the children's party,
> The prize awarded for the English Essay,
> The scholar's degree, the statesman's decoration.
> All things become less real, man passes
> From unreality to unreality.
> This man is obstinate, blind, intent
> On self-destruction,
> Passing from deception to deception,
> From grandeur to grandeur to final illusion,
> Lost in the wonder of his own greatness
> The enemy of society, enemy of himself.[11]

Clearly, this view of character is not entirely the creation of the twentieth century. Rather, it represents the intensification of perspectives which have been present throughout the

10. In the collection *One Arm and Other Stories,* pp. 9–10.

11. T. S. Eliot, *Murder in the Cathedral* (New York: Harcourt, Brace and Company, 1935), Act I, pp. 41–42; copyright 1935, by Harcourt, Brace & World, Inc., and reprinted with their permission.

history of Western letters. Albert Camus observes that much of existentialist dogma parallels the fundamental teachings of Jesus Christ. Certainly there are clear correspondences between existential teleologies and New Testament pronouncements on man's guilt, his search for truth, and his need for faith. Expressionism, existential theory, and "radical" Christian theology are agreed that man may find salvation only in love—in sympathy for his fellow man. Williams finds, then, considerable support for his vision of humanity from Christian theology and existential philosophy, as well as from the modern arts. His anti-hero is the symbol of a widely recognized condition: a "sickness unto death." Like the classic protagonist, the anti-hero searches for a mode of healing. But unlike the earlier protagonist he does not expect to find it. That which forbids his immediate salvation is himself. For the anti-hero is possessed of a profound fault, not merely of a single flaw, but of a comprehensive condition of evil, an inner impurity far greater than the Greek *hamartia*. Albérès describes this inner condition as "original sin."

The playwright gives shape to his anti-hero through the manipulation of a mythic glass; that is, Williams reveals his flawed image of man by showing his relationship to archetypal patterns. Throughout his work, Williams superimposes parallel visions—shadow images—of modern man. His anti-hero is a man of many identities; his Tom a "Hamlet," his Catharine a "Cassandra," his Brick an "Orestes," his Big Daddy an "Agamemnon." In *Orpheus Descending* his use of this technique of multiple vision is vivid. The Orphic figure Val descends into the underworld of Williams' mythical Mississippi town and there is brought to destruction by reveling maenads—Vee, Carol, and Lady—who envy his strange and magical music. Perhaps less obvious is Williams' use of a simultaneous treatment of character in *A Streetcar Named Desire*. Blanche—the poetic figure—descends into the underworld described as

"The Elysian Fields." The symbology is set forth in the protagonist's opening speech (Scene I, p. 11): "They told me to take a street-car named Desire, and then transfer to one called Cemeteries and ride six blocks and get off at—Elysian Fields!" In the critical scene preceding Blanche's destruction, Williams gives Orphic voice to the night:

> [. . . *The night is filled with inhuman voices like cries in a jungle.*
> [*The shadows and lurid reflections move sinuously as flames along the wall spaces.*
> [*Through the back wall of the rooms, which have become transparent, can be seen the sidewalk. . . .*] (Scene X, p. 148)

There is in this work a second source of character interpretation which, like the Orphic myth, has its major presentation in Greek mythology. Williams has found one of the antecedents for his anti-hero in the figure of the Euripidean Orestes. The Oresteian protagonist, like the contemporary image, is an anti-hero. He is a symbol of man in flight from the consequences of his own transgression, in search of his identity in the universe. Modern European dramatists, for reasons associated with their own intellectual history, have been more inclined to develop studies of the Aeschylean pre-tragic protagonist Prometheus. Throughout the work of Sartre, Anouilh, and Camus we see the outline of Prometheus in revolt against cosmic law. H. D. F. Kitto describes "Promethean heroism":

> We may now inquire what is the relation of Aristotle's theory to Aeschylus. The answer is roughly, None whatever. Aristotle's tragic hero, who must be neither good nor bad, but average (or a little better) and "like" us, is the Sophoclean hero who in himself prefigures the human tragedy, all of it. . . . The Aeschylean hero, who is not intended to sum up and typify in his own breast the tragic strength and weakness of man, need not be a blend and therefore cannot be "like" us; he must be only the sinner with so much characterization as to make him intelligible.[12]

The Americans, on the contrary, have been attracted to the late tragic apprehension of Euripides, especially by his images

12. H. D. F. Kitto, *Greek Tragedy: A Literary Study* (rev. ed.; New York, 1954), p. 116.

of Orpheus, Electra, Medea, and Orestes. While O'Neill reflects a certain interest in "Promethean man" in plays such as *Mourning Becomes Electra* and *Lazarus Laughed,* Williams, Miller, Inge, and, more recently, Albee conceive a protagonist closely akin to the anti-heroic image of Euripides.

The differences between these two apprehensions are significant. Promethean anti-heroism is revolutionary in nature. The pre-tragic protagonist of Aeschylus is, like Milton's Satan, a rebel: he is a creature in revolt against a powerful and inscrutable divinity. Albérès describes this Promethean anti-heroism:

> A man raises himself among other men. He sets himself up, by the requirement that he chooses to follow in a total solitude, social and metaphysical. . . . They [the heroes] wish to be alone, and it is in this sense that they refuse, from the beginning, the solutions of other men, the guaranteed, proven solutions. . . . Solitude defines the conditions of the hero, and his heroism is that he has not been born to accept the help of proven formulae. Prometheus is alone because he is the only one to dare, and his solitude expresses only the audacity of his enterprise.[13]

The Oresteian hero, treated in Aeschylus' trilogy, comes into sharper focus in the work of Euripides. For Euripides' Orestes —undoubtedly a fragment of a longer study—is the product of a particularly modern sensibility. Orestes is not a tragic hero in the Sophoclean tradition. He is, rather, an image of man concerned with his own power, responsibility, and complicity in the evil of the universe. Unlike the Sophoclean hero, the Euripidean anti-hero is himself the microcosm of universal evil as well as the image of universal good.

In an eloquent essay on Greek tragedy, Edith Hamilton attributes the continuing appeal of the Euripidean anti-hero for writers to the timeless nature of this playwright's perception. She describes Euripides as the "first modern mind." Miss Hamilton suggests that Euripides, writing at a point of crisis in Athenian history, was compelled to formulate answers to many of the problems which now confront the contemporaries: a

13. Albérès, pp. 125–26.

decline in religious faith, the acceleration of knowledge, political crises, and shifting moral values. She describes the peculiarly modern consciousness of the Greek dramatist:

He feels, as no other writer has felt, the pitifulness of human life, as of children suffering helplessly what they do not know and can never understand. . . . Out of the pages written more than twenty-three hundred years ago sound the two notes which we feel are the dominants in our world today, sympathy with suffering and the conviction of the worth of everyone alive. . . .

There is an order of mind which is perpetually modern. All of those possessed of it are akin, no matter how great the lapse of time that separates them. . . .

Always those in the vanguard of their time find in Euripides an expression of their own spirit. He is the great exponent of the forever recurring modern mind.[14]

Miss Hamilton describes Euripidean anti-heroism in terms which might well apply to the contemporary protagonist of Tennessee Williams:

Above all, they [the modern minds] care for human life and human things and can never stand aloof from them. They suffer for mankind, and what preoccupies them is the problem of pain. They are peculiarly sensitized to "the giant agony of the world." What they see as needless misery around them and what they envisage as needless misery to come is intolerable to them. The world to them is made up of individuals, each with a terrible power to suffer. . . .[15]

She traces the roots of the anti-heroic perception:

They behold, first and foremost, that most sorrowful thing on earth, injustice, and they are driven to it by a passion of revolt. Convention, so often a mask for injustice, they will have none of; in their pursuit of justice at any cost they tear away veils that hide hateful things: they call into question all pleasant and comfortable things. They are not of those who take "all life as their province"; what is good in the age they live in they do not regard; their eyes are fixed upon what is wrong. . . .[16]

---

14. Edith Hamilton, *The Greek Way to Western Civilization* (New York, 1948), pp. 197–98.
15. *Ibid.*, p. 199.
16. *Loc. cit.*

The Oresteian anti-hero is not, then, the virtuous man of Aristotelian description; he is, on the contrary, the symbol of a guilty humanity, the distillation of a fatal weakness in man. He cries out:

> O! human nature, what a grievous curse thou art in this world! and what salvation, too, to those who have a goodly heritage therein! [17]

Moreover, Orestes is a transgressor whose sins are supported, rather than diminished, by intelligence. For his fault is his lack of human compassion. While the gods have indeed preordained the punishment of Clytemnestra for the murder of Agamemnon, Orestes makes a free choice to act as her executioner. The brutal manner of his crime—a murder devoid of pity, calculated in vengeance, and executed without a trace of compassion—strikes horror even in the heartless gods. Orestes thus demonstrates a capacity for evil which is anti-human in its very aspect. Jean-Paul Sartre, in his modernization of the Euripidean legend, describes Orestes as a man who defies the gods in order to assume full responsibility in the universe:

> Foreign to myself—I know it. Outside nature, against nature, without excuse, beyond remedy, except what remedy I find within myself. But I shall not return under your law; I am doomed to have no other law but mine. Nor shall I come back to Nature, the Nature you found good; in it are a thousand beaten paths all leading up to you—but I must blaze my trail. For I, Zeus, am a man, and every man must find out his own way. . . .[18]

It is, then, primarily in consequence of his own choice that Orestes suffers. How does he suffer? The sophisticated dramatist Euripides, living at the beginning of the decline of the Greek Empire, saw in the sense of guilt a more ruinous form of pain than any devised by the gods or by man's enemies. In the opening scene of his *Orestes,* he portrays a man whose body is wracked by this corrosive inner disease: guilt. Orestes dem-

17. Euripides *Orestes,* trans. E. P. Coleridge, in *The Complete Greek Drama,* eds. Whitney J. Oates and Eugene O'Neill, Jr. (New York, 1938), II, 114.

18. Jean-Paul Sartre, *The Flies* in *No Exit and Three Other Plays,* trans. Stuart Gilbert (New York, 1955), p. 122.

onstrates all the symptoms of spiritual disintegration that afflict the modern anti-hero: the malaise, the fevered hallucinations, and the attacks of rage.[19] For his consciousness of transgression, Orestes pays the penalty of fragmentation, disorientation, and despair.

Orestes, clearly a more highly developed protagonist than the more primitive Agamemnon, suffers not for the existence of sin in the universe but for his consciousness of his own error. In Aeschylus' treatment of the subject, Orestes' madness has been prophesied by the Furies:

> Woe on you, younger gods! the ancient right
> Ye have o'erriden, rent it from my hands.
> I am dishonored of you, thrust to scorn!
> But heavily my wrath
> Shall on this land fling forth the drops that blast and burn,
> Venom of vengeance, that shall work such scathe
> As I have suffered; where that dew shall fall,
> Shall leafless blight arise,
> Wasting Earth's offspring—Justice, hear my call!—
> And thorough [through] all the land in deadly wise
> Shall scatter venom, to exude again
> In pestilence on men.[20]

In Euripides' *Electra*, the curse of the Furies is conveyed to Orestes by the Dioscuri:

> [B]ut haste thee to Athens, seeking to escape these hounds of hell, for they are on thy track in fearful wise, swart monsters, with snakes for hands, who reap a harvest of man's agony.[21]

The Euripidean myth, like the drama of Williams, is concerned not merely with defining the nature of sin; it seeks to find a human answer to suffering. Aeschylus, consistent with his theological orientation, summons man before the gods, where accused humanity is given a suspended sentence, a conditional acquittal. Euripides, on the other hand, places the re-

19. The indebtedness of Freud to Euripides is clearly illustrated in this work.
20. Aeschylus *Eumenides*, in *The Complete Greek Drama*, I, 298–99.
21. Euripides *Electra*, in *The Complete Greek Drama*, II, 105.

sponsibility for evil fully on man and challenges him to find a solution for the ills of his world.

The image of the anti-heroic Orestes seems always to have been present in the transgression-conscious American literature.[22] It is a clear motif in works such as *The Scarlet Letter, Billy Budd,* and *Moby Dick* as well as in William Faulkner's Euripidean studies of the mythical South. The Oresteian myth is a more subtly defined element of interpretation in the work of other Americans: in that of Walt Whitman, Robert Frost, T. S. Eliot, Emily Dickinson, and Edna St. Vincent Millay. In the works of all of these writers there appears the contour of the guilty protagonist, *man in exile,* in flight from his own transgression. D. H. Lawrence has commented that the study of guilt—the residue of the Puritan heritage—is one of the most persistent themes in American literature.[23] But the theme of metaphysical guilt is also an important element of modern European literature. The anti-hero of Tennessee Williams belongs to the lineage of Shakespeare, Goethe, Dostoevski, Gide, Kafka, and Thomas Mann, as well as to that of Hawthorne, Melville, and Faulkner. Like these writers, Williams explores one of the most persistent themes in modern letters: the significance of human transgression.

In order to examine this metaphysical problem, Williams sets in motion an anti-heroic cycle of human experience. Like Dante's poet, his anti-hero traverses the downward way in his "dark night of the soul."[24] Blanche, in *A Streetcar Named Desire,* describes her descent in the spiritual cycle:

22. See Doris Falk, *Eugene O'Neill and The Tragic Tension* (New Brunswick, New Jersey, 1958).

23. See D. H. Lawrence, *Studies in Classic American Literature* (New York, 1923).

24. The Bochum critics thought Dante to be among Williams' strongest influences, especially in *Camino Real.*

There are thousands of papers, stretching back over hundreds of years, affecting Belle Reve as, piece by piece, our improvident grandfathers and father and uncles and brothers exchanged the land for their epic fornications—to put it plainly! . . . The four-letter word deprived us of our plantation, till finally all that was left—and Stella can verify that!—was the house itself and about twenty acres of ground, including a graveyard, to which now all but Stella and I have retreated. (Scene II, p. 45)

Blanche, in her downward progress toward salvation, comes to the realization of her own responsibility for suffering. She becomes aware that she suffers more for her own transgressions than for the actions of her guilty ancestors. Like Orestes, she has made a guilty choice: a choice which has involved her in the suffering of others. She suggests that she is the effective cause of her husband's death. In her moment of partial "enlightenment" she describes the critical moment when she withdrew "sympathy" from a morally helpless being:

He'd stuck the revolver into his mouth, and fired—so that the back of his head had been—blown away!

It was because—on the dance-floor—unable to stop myself—I'd suddenly said—"I saw! I know! You disgust me . . ." And then the searchlight which had been turned on the world was turned off again and never for one moment since has there been any light that's stronger than this—kitchen—candle. (Scene VI, pp. 109–10)

Blanche records her descent into the hell of suffering. She describes her agony:

I, I, *I* took the blows in my face and my body! All of those deaths! The long parade to the graveyard! . . . And funerals are pretty compared to deaths. . . . You didn't dream, but I saw! *Saw, Saw!* And now you sit there telling me with your eyes that I let the place go! How in hell do you think all that sickness and dying was paid for? Death is expensive, Miss Stella! . . . (Scene I, pp. 25–26)

The play begins at a point late in the development of the anti-heroic cycle. In his record of this movement, Williams exposes Blanche's progressive fragmentation, her progress toward the last circle of hell. In *A Streetcar Named Desire,* Williams concludes his development at the ultimate point of descent; that is to say, this play closes without a clear resolution.

If his earlier works trace the protagonist's descent into the private hell of consciousness, it is only in later plays that Williams begins the description of the long and torturous ascent of the anti-hero to a limited enlightenment. We see some hint of resolution in *Summer and Smoke* in the redemption of Dr. John by the young and lovely Nellie. Similarly, in *Cat on a Hot Tin Roof*—a vivid transposition of the Oresteian myth—there is some suggestion of hope in the renewed bonds of sympathy between the dying father and son, as well as in the possibility of a new life which may cancel out old sins. A second movement—the ascent to light—is more clearly marked in *Camino Real,* a play in which Williams offers, as savior of mankind, the American soldier of fortune Kilroy, a protagonist who redeems the world with a simple display of sympathy. A more complete cycle of understanding is suggested in *The Night of the Iguana,* where the world-weary Shannon finds God through the friendship of Hannah, a woman who offers him sympathy.

A review of the whole body of Williams' work would seem to indicate that the playwright has not as yet completely resolved the problem of reconciliation in his cycle of anti-heroic development. He has succeeded in stating the case against man, in describing his anti-heroic condition. Moreover, he has formulated the general outlines of a kind of virtue appropriate to this condition. His greatest achievement, perhaps, is his definition of present conditions of heroism. For in his drama the anti-hero engages himself to suffer the agony of conscience, to confront hidden truth, and to accept the heavy burden of metaphysical guilt. Blanche, Alma, Brick, Kilroy, Chance, Val, Catharine, and Shannon may be described in these terms:

That which distinguishes the character from those who surround him is that a problem poses itself for him, a problem which others ignore or dare not confront; it is that he is more and more tormented. None of these persons who have attracted our great writers is remarkable in the sense of those who have preceded them. They are men like others, but they ask themselves certain questions while others allow themselves to live.[25]

If the willingness to engage inner conflict is the nature of heroism in the theatre of Williams, his organization of character is designed to reveal such action by exploring, in relation to the protagonist, the full range of possibilities affecting his moral choice. The anti-hero, in this sense, is not a man; he is a schematic presentation of extended moral possibilities. In each of his characters Williams presents a composite image, a montage of the roles which together comprise the anti-heroic character. Alma, in *Summer and Smoke,* speaks of this view of character:

I've thought many times of something you told me last summer, that I have a *doppleganger*. I looked that up and I found that it means another person inside of me, another self, and I don't know whether to thank you or not for making me conscious of it!—I haven't been well. . . . For a while I thought I was dying, that that was the change that was coming. (Scene XI, p. 115)

In his presentation of character, Williams follows the method of exposition which in modern theatre is associated with the theories of Luigi Pirandello. For Pirandello defined dramatic character as an agglomeration of roles:

For the drama lies all in this—in the conscience that I have, that each one of us has. We believe this conscience to be a single thing, but it is many-sided. There is one for this person, and another for that. Diverse consciences. So we have this illusion of being one person for all, of having a personality that is unique in all our acts. But it isn't true. We perceive this when, tragically perhaps, in something we do, we are as it were, suspended, caught up in the air on a kind of hook. Then we perceive that all of us was not in that act, and that it would be an atrocious injustice to judge us by that action alone. . . .[26]

25. Albérès, p. 125.
26. Luigi Pirandello, *Six Characters in Search of an Author* in *Naked Masks: Five Plays,* ed. Eric Bentley, trans. E. Storer (New York, 1952), p. 231–32.

In this theory, Pirandello attempted to provide for modern drama a concept of character consistent with the relative perspective of twentieth-century thought: to create an image of man in all of his complexity, in the full reality of his inner disharmony. It is important to observe that Pirandello's theory corresponds not only to the relative vision of artists such as Picasso, but also to that of the great creative thinkers such as Jung.[27] Like Jungian psychology, Pirandello's theory defines character as a loosely unified grouping of identities. Pirandellian Man, like Jungian Man, is a configuration of masks. He is an image of man in search of a reconciling symbol, in need of a self above selves.

This pattern of organization, despite its intellectual validity, presents serious theatrical problems. How can such a concept of character be realized in the sensible form of the drama? European playwrights such as Brecht have solved this problem by introducing into the drama large quantities of discursive material. They explain the conflicted nature of the protagonist's character through the use of monologues, films, notes, and other "teaching devices." Americans such as O'Neill and Miller have also on occasion used such techniques. Although Williams makes some use of the interior monologue, he has been inclined to figure inner conflict in more theatrical terms. He follows the example of Shakespeare in revealing character through schematic arrangement. Like Hamlet, Blanche DuBois reveals her inner nature by playing out her conflicted roles: schoolteacher, Southern belle, poet, sister, savior, and prostitute. Similarly, Alma, Brick, Quixote, Chance, Val, Shannon, and others play out a range of characters, as they don first one mask and then another.

Although it was interpreted by Pirandello, this idea of character development should be credited to Shakespeare. Indeed, it may be described as the "Hamlet organization": for the anti-

27. This Jungian language also seems to be employed by Pirandello. The relationship between Jung and Pirandello has not, to my knowledge, been fully explored.

Tennessee Williams on the Broadway set of
A Streetcar Named Desire (courtesy *Life* Magazine)

In a play, time is arrested in the sense of being confined. . . . The audience can sit back in the comforting dusk to watch a world which is flooded with light and in which emotion and action have a dimension and dignity that they would likewise have in real existence, if only the shattering intrusion of time could be locked out.

Preface to the *Rose Tattoo,* p. ix

The Broadway production of *A Streetcar Named Desire* (courtesy Graphic House, Inc.)

The audience at the beginning should . . . want Stanley to tell her off. He does. He exposes her and then gradually, as they see how genuinely in pain, how actually desperate she is . . . they begin . . . to realize that they are sitting in at the death of something extraordinary . . . and then they feel the tragedy.

Elia Kazan, "Notebook for *A Streetcar Named Desire*" in *Directing the Play*, p. 299

And in my dissident opinion, a play in a book is only a shadow of a play and not even a clear shadow of it. Those who did not like *Camino Real* on the stage will not be likely to form a high opinion of it in print, for of all the works I have written, this one was meant most for the vulgarity of performance.

Preface to *Camino Real,* p. xii

The Broadway production of *Camino Real* (courtesy Alfredo Valente)

Big Daddy (Burl Ives) in *Cat on a Hot Tin Roof* (photograph courtesy Graphic House, Inc.)

The bird that I hope to catch in the net of this play is not the solution of one man's psychological problem. I'm trying to catch the true quality of experience in a group of people, that cloudy, flickering, evanescent—fiercely charged!—interplay of live human beings in the thundercloud of a common crisis.

Stage directions in *Cat on a Hot Tin Roof*, Act II, p. 98

Princess and Chance (Geraldine Page and Paul Newman) in *Sweet Bird of Youth* (photograph courtesy Graphic House, Inc.)

[I]f there is any truth in the Aristotelian idea that violence is purged by its poetic representation on the stage, then it may be that my cycle of violent plays have had a moral justification after all.

Preface to *Sweet Bird of Youth*, p. xi

heroic Hamlet is perhaps the most effective theatrical example of this multiple concept of human personality. Hamlet is organized from simultaneous visions in much the manner of the modern anti-hero. Shakespeare rationalized his use of montage by attributing to his protagonist the consciousness of an actor. Mark Van Doren describes Hamlet's character as a "spectacle forever suspended":

> Hamlet is an actor. Like any character in whom Shakespeare was greatly interested, he plays a role. He plays indeed many roles, being supreme in tragedy as Falstaff was supreme in comedy. . . . Like Falstaff he shows the man he is by being many men. . . . He acts with the King and Queen, with Ophelia, with Polonius, with the court at large; taking on and putting off each role as occasion dictates, and at the climax of the tragedy wearing all of them simultaneously.[28]

Shakespeare, then, revealed the nature of Hamlet's character by exposing the possibilities of *action* and *being* contingent upon a moment of choice. In the course of his time upon the stage, Hamlet plays many roles; he is alternately prince and jester, lover and knave, courtier and politician, poet and ribald jester.

A study of the work of Williams would seem to show that he takes this "existential" Hamlet as his point of departure in his organization of anti-heroic character. For he seeks to affirm in character the present; his protagonists have little real past and no hope for a future. They are locked within a moment of choice. The form of Williams is thus a record of a critical instant in individual destiny. The stage for action is consciousness: it is a consciousness filled with spectres who are in effect extensions of the self. This principle is perhaps most clearly demonstrated in *The Night of the Iguana,* one of his latest plays. Here, as in other works, Williams creates a mythical way station in his progression of understanding. To this "point" he brings a number of characters, each personifying a particular virtue or vice in the consciousness of the protagonist. The aged poet is at one extreme of the continuum. A man who has lost

28. Mark Van Doren, ed., Introduction to *Four Great Tragedies* (New York, 1955), p. 208.

the will to live, he is countered by a young and eager girl. The energetic German family is posed against the casual Mexicans; the corrupt agent Latta against the anti-heroic Shannon; the saintly Hannah against the "insatiable widow" Maxine. *The Night of the Iguana* is a kind of modern *Everyman,* a moment when the protagonist watches his own vices and virtues parade across the great stage of his consciousness.

A more subtle use of the Hamlet device may be seen in an earlier work, *The Glass Menagerie.* For Williams creates in this drama a conscious self: the observing and reflecting "Tom" who projects the flow of experience from his own recall. Within his stream of consciousness there exists another "Tom," the acting self. As the play progresses, it becomes evident that each of the other members of Tom's family represents a position in his pattern of understanding. *The Glass Menagerie,* like O'Neill's *The Great God Brown,* is an exploration of life possibilities, a review of the roles conceived by an anti-heroic man. In *The Glass Menagerie* Williams conceives three of these masks: that of Amanda, the self of natural life; of Laura, the self of poetry and illusion; and of the father, the self of action. Tom explains his choice of a life role in these words,

> I didn't go to the moon, I went much further—for time is the longest distance between two places—. . . .
>
> I left Saint Louis. I descended the steps of this fire-escape for a last time and followed, from then on, in my father's footsteps. . . .
>
> (Scene VIII, p. 123)

In *The Glass Menagerie,* as in the other major works of Tennessee Williams, the protagonist pursues his "odyssey," his journey toward selfhood. Within the "lyric instant," the moment of escape from the corrosive life process, the protagonist conducts his search for a principle through which he may bring meaning to experience. He does this by exploring the alternatives mirrored within this image of his own consciousness. Williams thus examines a comprehensive theme of twentieth-century arts, the search for identity: the journey toward meaning. It is because of his perception of a moral crisis that Williams has abandoned more flattering images of man. Apparently shocked and frightened by the growing threat of human annihilation, he suggests that the theatre cannot afford to exalt man, to praise and to commend his nature. He insists that the proper function of the modern drama is to expose man's hidden nature, to search out his motives, to discover his limits, and, ultimately, to help him to find a mode of salvation. There is little doubt that in his anti-hero Williams states the case against modern man effectively. However, he has been able to evolve only a limited resolution for his cycle of suffering. He concludes that the only hope for man is compassion. It is love that redeems the damned city of Camino Real and sets the "water to flowing again in the mountains."

The anti-heroic protagonist of Williams is designed to reveal the nature of suffering as it appears in the life of the twentieth century. He is intended as the object of pity and terror in the modern world. A question is often asked about this aspect of Williams' work: Of what meaning is the fate of his emotional, spiritual, and moral cripples? The answer given by Williams reflects the gradual usurpation of the pagan idea of tragedy by the Christian concept of human worth. For the Christian ethic holds every man a sinner, redeemable only through love. Similarly, it insists, as does Williams, that all men are anti heroic; that these figures, no more than others, are guilty of the human condition. In this context, Williams' catalogue of transgressors in search of salvation is a true symbolism—is anti-hero, the very present image of man.

chapter five

THE PLASTIC THEATRE

Williams and his artistic collaborators, Margo Jones, Jo Mielziner, Jean Rosenthal, Lee Strasberg, Elia Kazan, and others, have given to plays such as *The Glass Menagerie, A Streetcar Named Desire,* and *Camino Real* a production form known in world theatre as the "American method."[1] This American

1. This "American method" should be distinguished from the "Stanislavskian method," from which it is in part derived. Although many of the American innovators began by studying and imitating the theories of the Russian *metteur en scène,* certain major alterations have been effected which give to the American drama a character distinct from that of earlier forms. Artists such as Elia Kazan have contributed to the modification of the psychological naturalism of Stanislavsky. Kazan employs elements of the expressionistic techniques of Piscator, Brecht, and others; as well as components of the formalism of Craig, Vakhtangov, Meyerhold, and Copeau; and the symbolism of Wagner, Appia, Nemirovich-Danchenko and Yeats. Moreover, Kazan

method is characterized by its own distinctive style of directing as well as by its own patterns of acting, staging, designing, and lighting. Indeed, it is possible that one of Williams' most lasting achievements may be his contribution to the development of this American dramaturgy, to the creation of this distinctive production form.

From the beginning of his career, Williams has been engaged in the formulation of a dramaturgy for his theatre. He describes his dramatic text as a series of notations—a score—set down by a composer. His rejection of the play manuscript as complete drama is based on his belief in the surrealistic nature of poetic expression. Like Wagner, he suggests that much of the significant content of drama is suprarational in nature and, in consequence, extra-verbal in form. His "plastic theatre" is concerned not only with the exposition of rational planes of experience but also with the connotation of the ambiguous world of meaning above and below accepted levels of reason. Williams attempts to project into the cube called a "stage" a vision of the entire complex of human experience, including those planes of reality which Wagner described as "unutterable." Like Wagner, the playwright found early in his career that this motive requires a more sensitive instrument than ordinary speech. Following Wagner and his symbolist disciples, Williams has attempted to restore to the theatre a more complete theatrical syntax.

Williams, as an American, has assumed another related responsibility: that of building a theatrical language capable of connoting the distinctive American consciousness. Examples of

---

and his associates have infused into the plastic form, as Williams has into the literary drama, the spirit of the American popular arts. The production form and stage design of a work such as *A Streetcar Named Desire* borrow heavily from the common forms of American life: from cinema, newspaper, and magazine; from television and billboards; and from illustrations and advertisements. The acting style, codified and formalized by Kazan, Clurman, Lee Strasberg, and others—the style of Actors' Studio—was designed to provide a mode of physical expression congruent with American drama and scene design.

his early experimentation with this problem may be seen in the short works of the series 27 *Wagons Full of Cotton* and *American Blues*. Williams, in these plays, began the development of the expository technique for which he would in later years become famous. In plays such as *The Purification* he integrates elements of traditional American music, dance, recitation, and mime. Moreover, he projects these symbolic structures against a background which borrows components of its textural form from American painting, architecture, and sculpture as well as from the cinema. These early plays exist somewhere between theatre forms. They are part ballet, part recitation, part cinema, and part tableau. Like the modern American dance theatre, they are articulated in a language which extends across those boundaries which in recent centuries have separated the performing arts. *The Purification,* for example, requires for its explication a highly versatile company: a guitar player, a pantomimist, a speech choir, dancers, and a large cast, fluent in movement and in the speaking of poetry.

Early in his career Williams came to the theoretical rejection of realism. Some of his anti-realist tendencies may be traced to his studies at the New School for Social Research which was, during his tenure, the home of the great expressionist director Erwin Piscator. During the early forties Piscator directed a number of critically outstanding productions, including Bertolt Brecht's *The Caucasian Chalk Circle* and Shakespeare's *King Lear*. It seems likely that Piscator's "epic" theatre influenced the young playwright; for in 1945, Williams published, as a preface to *The Glass Menagerie,* an expressionist-oriented manifesto. He presents in this document a well-developed theory of form. He describes his theatre in these anti-realist terms:

> Being a "memory play," *The Glass Menagerie* can be presented with unusual freedom of convention. Because of its considerably delicate or tenuous material, atmospheric touches and subtleties of direction play a particularly important part. Expressionism and all other unconventional techniques in drama have only one valid aim, and that is a closer approach to truth. When a play employs unconventional techniques, it is not, or certainly shouldn't be, trying to escape its responsibility of dealing

with reality, or interpreting experience, but is actually or should be attempting to find a closer approach, a more penetrating and vivid expression of things as they are. The straight realistic play with its genuine frigidaire and authentic ice-cubes, its characters that speak exactly as its audience speaks, corresponds to the academic landscape and has the same virtue of a photographic likeness. Everyone should know nowadays the unimportance of the photographic in art: that truth, life, or reality is an organic thing which the poetic imagination can represent or suggest, in essence, only through transformation, through changing into other forms than those which were merely present in appearance.

These remarks are not meant as a preface only to this particular play. They have to do with a conception of a new, plastic theatre which must take the place of the exhausted theatre of realistic conventions if the theatre is to resume vitality as a part of our culture.

(Production Notes, p. ix)

In *The Glass Menagerie* Williams borrows heavily from the expressionists,[2] particularly from the "epic" form of Piscator and Brecht. Like Brecht, he employs a screen as the symbol of consciousness. His use of the screen for the projection of "memory" differs, however, from the Brechtian employment of the same device for the formulation of political and social ideographs. Williams proposes here to create a poetic image which is explicated through the figuration of lesser forms. The playwright describes these component images:

Each scene contains a particular point (or several) which is structurally the most important. In an episodic play, such as this, the basic structure or narrative line may be obscured from the audience; the effect may seem fragmentary rather than architectural. . . . The legend or image upon the screen will strengthen the effect of what is merely allusion in the writing and allow the primary point to be made more simply and lightly than if the entire responsibility were on the spoken lines. Aside from this structural value, I think the screen will have a definite emotional appeal, less definable but just as important.

(Production Notes, p. x)

The playwright describes the concept responsible for the creation of his plastic images. Like Brecht, he attempts to create a kind of theatre "language," a system of connotative signs.

2. Schlemmer and others, *The Theatre of the Bauhaus* (Middletown, Connecticut, 1961).

Unlike Brecht, however, Williams fills his language with dense emotive contents. He describes the use of music within his sensuous symbol:

> Another extra-literary accent in this play is provided by the use of music. A single recurring tune, "The Glass Menagerie," is used to give emotional emphasis to suitable passages. This tune is like circus music, not when you are on the grounds or in the immediate vicinity of the parade, but when you are at some distance and very likely thinking of something else. It seems under those circumstances to continue almost interminably and it weaves in and out of your preoccupied consciousness; then it is the lightest, most delicate music in the world and perhaps the saddest. It expresses the surface vivacity of life with the underlying strain of immutable and inexpressible sorrow. When you look at a piece of delicately spun glass you think of two things: how beautiful it is and how easily it can be broken. Both of those ideas should be woven into the recurring tune, which dips in and out of the play as if it were carried on a wind that changes. It serves as a thread of connection and allusion between the narrator with his separate point in time and space and the subject of his story. Between each episode it returns as reference to the emotion, nostalgia, which is the first condition of the play. It is primarily Laura's music and therefore comes out most clearly when the play focuses upon her and the lovely fragility of glass which is her image.
> (Production Notes, p. xi)

Williams attempts to create a theatre language of profound emotional intensity:

> THE LIGHTING
>
> The lighting in the play is not realistic. In keeping with the atmosphere of memory, the stage is dim. Shafts of light are focused on selected areas or actors, sometimes in contradistinction to what is the apparent center. For instance, in the quarrel scene between Tom and Amanda, in which Laura has no active part, the clearest pool of light is on her figure. This is also true of the supper scene, when her silent figure on the sofa should remain the visual center. The light upon Laura should be distinct from the others, having a peculiar pristine clarity such as light used in early religious portraits of female saints or madonnas. A certain correspondence to light in religious paintings, such as El Greco's, where the figures are radiant in atmosphere that is relatively dusky, could be effectively used throughout the play. (It will also permit a more effective use of the screen.) A free imaginative use of light can be of enormous

value in giving a mobile, plastic quality to plays of a more or less static nature. (Production Notes, pp. xi–xii)

Williams' theatre symbol, unlike the hard, gemlike form of Brecht, possesses textural quality. He describes his sensuous symbol as "plastic." The idea of a "plastic symbol," a form with the sculptural quality of "dimension," is not new. Prior to 1945, it appeared in the theories of the French symbolists and in the related ideas of the American imagists. A similar idea was responsible for the appearance of a whole rash of forms in the Dadaist movement of the early twenties. Insofar as the theatre is concerned, we recognize the "plastic symbol" as a variation on Wagner's concept of synthesis—a concept which has dominated much of twentieth-century theatrical practice. For Wagner, in revolt against the word-dominated theatre of the nineteenth century, the creation of a synthetic symbol represented an attempt to restore to drama a textural language—a theatrical grammar—which could give expression to irrational contents in experience. If Brecht attempted to "alienate" his symbol from such ambiguous contents, Williams, like Wagner, has been interested in giving shape to that very world of unnamable experience which Wagner described as "unutterable." Fergusson suggests that the idea of such a symbol has influenced the practice of Yeats, Eliot, O'Neill, Maeterlinck, Claudel, Cocteau, and Giraudoux, as well as the theories of Craig, Copeau, and Granville-Barker. We may also identify the plastic symbol in the theatre of the expressionists Meyerhold, Vakhtangov, and Komisarjevsky.[3] But the plastic symbol of Williams, while showing definite correspondences to these earlier forms, is in many ways a distinctive structure. It is a more flexible entity, a more ambiguous form.

If Wagner wished to subordinate all aesthetic components in his theatre to the authority of music, and if Craig attempted to impose the unity of vision upon all elements, Williams has structured a more balanced symbol. He has not, like Yeats, emphasized dance over spoken language, nor has he, like

3. Fergusson, *The Idea of a Theater* (Princeton, 1949), pp. 206–40.

Brecht, attempted to cut away all associative meanings from a "pure word." Plastic form in the theatre of Williams seems to rest on a synthesis of different proportions. In the language of the theorist Antonin Artaud, it is "poetry in space"; its architectonic structure is composed of "word, music, dance, plastic art, pantomime, mimicry, gesticulation, intonation, architecture, lighting, and scenery." [4]

A study of the body of Williams' dramatic work—both plays and essays—would seem to indicate that his idea of a plastic form has experienced at least three stages of growth. He describes his very early work as an attempt to bring into the theatre that "finely spun illusion" which is the artist's own vision. In the subsequent period of his development he seems to have structured a second level of interpretation; that is, he extended the scope of his primary poetic realization by posing above the level of pure feeling—and beneath it—more objective linguistic structures. If the early plays such as *This Property Is Condemned* are interesting because of the singularity of their interpretations, the later works such as *Summer and Smoke* are absorbing because they seem to suggest the employment of simultaneous linguistic structures. This complication of his interpretative symbol grows even more marked in plays of a later period—in *Camino Real, Suddenly Last Summer, Orpheus Descending, Sweet Bird of Youth,* and *The Night of the Iguana.*

One of the most interesting examples of Williams' early plastic form is *The Purification,* from the series 27 *Wagons Full of Cotton.* This drama bears a strong resemblance to certain of the choreographic studies of Martha Graham as well as to the ritual dance cycles of José Limón, Doris Humphrey, and Hanya Holm. *The Purification,* like these dance compositions, is designed to evoke a single poetic image, an image of the American Southwest. It is a theatre composition in which the key figure is

4. *The Theater and Its Double,* trans. Mary Caroline Richards (New York, 1958), p. 39.

the girl Elena. Her image rises from the instrument of an "Orpheus," the Guitar Player. Within this vision, lesser forms appear: the shape of love is balanced by an image of hate. Reason, symbolized by the Judge, is countered by primitive passion, given expression by a chorus. The play is the projection of poetic paradox: the illusion of love-in-hate, light-in-dark, death-in-life. Williams suggests structural tension within his poetic composition: words are aligned against music and gesture is more emphatic than speech. Significant to this discussion is the fact that the important moments in the fragmentary narrative are interpreted as dance. The girl herself appears but three times, and on two of these occasions she does not speak. The playwright describes her in these choreographic terms:

(Rosalio's sister, Elena of the Springs, steps into the doorway. She wears a sheer white robe and bears white flowers. With slender candle-like fingers she parts the shawl that covers her head and reveals her face. Her lips are smiling. But only The Son Rosalio is aware of the apparition —he and The Guitar Player. The others stare at the Indian woman, Luisa, who rises stiffly from the bench beside The Rancher from Casa Rojo.)

. . . .

(The girl of the vision lowers her head and covers her face and her garland with the shawl. The guitar plays—sad and sinister. She turns and withdraws from the doorway.)

(In *27 Wagons Full of Cotton,* p. 36)

Williams includes within the dialogue of this play his "apology" for the use of these expressive techniques. It is the protagonist who explains to the spectator (page 41) why truth cannot be communicated through words but must rather be suggested through music and dance. It is not surprising that *The Purification,* like *A Streetcar Named Desire,* has been transposed into dance theatre.[5] For its development is *lyric,* not

5. *The Purification,* choreographed by Mary Anthony, had its première at the White Barn Theatre, Westport, Connecticut, in August, 1957. The production is noted in *Dance,* XXXII (January, 1958), 70.

Ballet Theatre's production of *This Property Is Condemned* (1957) is noted in *Theatre Arts,* XLI (July, 1957), 80.

A Streetcar Named Desire, choreographed by Valerie Bettis, had its pre-

simply because it employs music and dance in the creation of its image, but because its subject is feeling: its mode of unity —its motif—is rhythm. The pattern of its dramatic development is established by the guitar; it is sustained and elaborated by the dancing and chanting chorus; it is brought to a shattering climax by the formalized dance duel in the closing moments of the play.

In the second period of his development—1948–1955—Williams elaborated this lyric pattern of expression in two ways. We have noted, in the context of an earlier discussion, that the dramatist has raised a rational superstructure above his lyric moment. This intellectual development has its theatric parallel. In *A Streetcar Named Desire, Summer and Smoke, The Rose Tattoo,* and *Cat on a Hot Tin Roof,* Williams provides scenic symbols of greater density. He gives to the composition of scenes a more sculptural quality as he manipulates form, volume, texture, line, color, light, shade, and space. A description of such a scene is given in *A Streetcar Named Desire:*

THE POKER NIGHT

There is a picture of Van Gogh's of a billiard-parlor at night. The kitchen now suggests that sort of lurid nocturnal brilliance, the raw colors of childhood's spectrum. Over the yellow linoleum of the kitchen table hangs an electric bulb with a vivid green glass shade. The poker players—Stanley, Steve, Mitch, and Pablo—wear colored shirts, solid blues, a purple, a red-and-white check, a light green, and they are men at the peak of their physical manhood, as coarse and direct and powerful

---

mière in New York in February, 1953. At that time, the role of Blanche was danced by Mia Slavenska. In its London production, the role of Blanche was danced by the dramatic American ballerina, Nora Kaye. For a review of that performance, see Joan Lawson, "Ballet Theatre in London," *Dancing Times,* LXVII (October, 1956), 17–19.

Miss Bettis is quoted as saying that Williams provides in this drama a rich vein of non-verbal content. Her choreography is developed along much the same lines described by Elia Kazan. Both attempt to find concrete symbols for the multiple reality of Williams' description. See Doris Hering, "Valerie Bettis Choreographs Streetcar Named Desire," *Dance,* XXVI (December, 1952), 21 and 59. A different assessment of this choreographic effort is given by a second writer. See Norma G. Stahl, "Converting Literature into Dance," *Dance,* XXVII (March, 1953), 16–18, 47.

as the primary colors. There are vivid slices of watermelon on the table, whiskey bottles and glasses. The bedroom is relatively dim with only the light that spills between the portieres and through the wide window on the street.

For a moment, there is absorbed silence as a hand is dealt.

(Scene III, p. 48)

Each of the plays in this second period is conceived by the dramatist as a visual composition, both as scenic design and as staging patterns. Among the most effective of these visual designs articulated by Williams are those suggested for *Summer and Smoke*. In his description of the setting, Williams gives explication to a central metaphor—to the divided consciousness of Western man, the tension between body and soul:

There are two of these "interior" sets, one being the parlor of an Episcopal Rectory and the other the home of a doctor next door to the Rectory. The architecture of these houses is barely suggested but is of an American Gothic design of the Victorian era. There are no actual doors or windows or walls. Doors and windows are represented by delicate frameworks of Gothic design. These frames have strings of ivy clinging to them, the leaves of emerald and amber. Sections of wall are used only where they are functionally required. There should be a fragment of wall in back of the Rectory sofa, supporting a romantic landscape in a gilt frame. In the doctor's house there should be a section of wall to support the chart of anatomy. Chirico has used fragmentary walls and interiors in a very evocative way in his painting called "Conversation among the Ruins."

(Production Notes, Scene I, pp. viii–ix)

Williams employs in this passage one of his characteristic techniques: that of transposing the interpretative forms of the painting arts into the theatre. In *Summer and Smoke* he tells us that he has been influenced by the symbolic language of the Italian "metaphysical abstractionist" Giorgio de Chirico. In *A Streetcar Named Desire* he employs the raw coloring and primitive forms of the Fauves—particularly those of Van Gogh—as the visual equivalents of his universe. In *The Glass Menagerie* he invokes El Greco, while *Camino Real, Orpheus Descending,* and *Suddenly Last Summer* are surrealist visions which borrow from the symbolism of Dali, Max Ernst, and Odilon Redon. The opening scene for *Suddenly Last Summer* is described in the following way:

> *The set may be as unrealistic as the decor of a dramatic ballet. It represents part of a mansion of Victorian Gothic style in the Garden District of New Orleans on a late afternoon, between late summer and early fall. The interior is blended with a fantastic garden which is more like a tropical jungle, or forest, in the prehistoric age of giant fern-forests when living creatures had flippers turning to limbs and scales to skin. The colors of this jungle-garden are violent, especially since it is steaming with heat after rain. There are massive tree-flowers that suggest organs of a body, torn out, still glistening with undried blood; there are harsh cries and sibilant hissings and thrashing sounds in the garden as if it were inhabited by beasts, serpents and birds, all of savage nature. . . .*
>
> . . . .
>
> *A lady enters with the assistance of a silver-knobbed cane. She has light orange or pink hair and wears a lavender lace dress, and over her withered bosom is pinned a starfish of diamonds.*
>
> *She is followed by a young blond Doctor, all in white, glacially brilliant, very, very good looking. . . .* (Scene I, p. 13–14)

All of the symbols of Williams' scenic vision are not surrealist in nature.[6] In *Sweet Bird of Youth,* he conceives his setting after the manner of the American painter, Georgia O'Keeffe.

> *The terrace of* BOSS FINLEY'S *house, which is a frame house of Victorian Gothic design, suggested by a door frame at the right and a single white column. As in the other scenes, there are no walls, the action occurring against the sky and sea cyclorama.*
>
> *The Gulf is suggested by the brightness and the gulls crying as in Act One. There is only essential porch furniture, Victorian wicker but painted bone white. The men should also be wearing white or off-white suits: the tableau is all blue and white, as strict as a canvas of Georgia O'Keeffe's.* (Act II, Scene 1, p. 46)

In Act II, Scene 2, of the same play, Williams employs television, a new visual form, as an element of his image. In a montage, a simultaneous presentation of action, he exploits this device:

6. See Herbert Read, *The Philosophy of Modern Art,* pp. 110–54.

[STUFF *makes a gesture as if to turn on the TV, which we play in the fourth wall. A wavering beam of light, flickering, narrow, intense, comes from the balcony rail.* STUFF *moves his head so that he's in it, looking into it. . . .* CHANCE *walks slowly downstage, his head also in the narrow flickering beam of light. As he walks downstage, there suddenly appears on the big TV screen, which is the whole back wall of the stage, the image of* BOSS FINLEY. *His arm is around* HEAVENLY *and he is speaking. . . . When* CHANCE *sees the* BOSS'S *arm around* HEAVENLY, *he makes a noise in his throat like a hard fist hit him low. . . . Now the sound, which always follows the picture by an instant, comes on . . . loud.*] (Act II, Scene 2, p. 96)

In his late work, Williams continues to integrate other visual forms into his plastic symbol. He describes an eighteenth-century masque as an element of the action in *Sweet Bird of Youth:*

[CHARLES *turns on a coach lamp by the door. This marks a formal division in the scene. The light change is not realistic; the light doesn't seem to come from the coach lamp but from a spectral radiance in the sky, flooding the terrace.*

[The sea wind sings. HEAVENLY *lifts her face to it. Later that night may be stormy, but now there is just a quickness and freshness coming in from the Gulf.* HEAVENLY *is always looking that way, toward the Gulf, so that the light from Point Lookout catches her face with its repeated soft stroke of clarity.*

[In her father, a sudden dignity is revived. Looking at his very beautiful daughter, he becomes almost stately. He approaches her, [as] *soon as the colored man returns inside, like an aged courtier comes deferentially up to a Crown Princess or Infanta. It's important not to think of his attitude toward her in the terms of crudely conscious incestuous feeling, but just in the natural terms of almost any aging father's feeling for a beautiful young daughter who reminds him of a dead wife that he desired intensely when she was the age of his daughter.*

[At this point there might be a phrase of stately, Mozartian music, suggesting a court dance. The flagged terrace may suggest the parquet floor of a ballroom and the two players' movements may suggest the stately, formal movements of a court dance of that time; but if this effect is used, it should be just a suggestion. The change toward "stylization" ought to be held in check.] (Act II, Scene 1, pp. 56–57)

The playwright employs a highly articulate visual language through which he gives concrete shape to his poetic perception. But the plastic theatre of Williams is not confined to visual structures. Its sensuous symbol also embraces sound patterns: words, music, and aural effects. Williams scores his middle dramas with elaborately orchestrated compositions, with intricate patterns of songs, voices, music, noises, and cries. In *A Streetcar Named Desire* the key image in this aural composition—a montage that arises from the consciousness of Blanche—is a "blue piano" which, Williams writes, embodies the spirit of the play. Around it the playwright develops a fabric of sound. This pattern of images is elaborated in *Cat on a Hot Tin Roof,* where every stage in the dramatic progression is illustrated by sound, and where each character has his own aural motif.

Williams describes the sound of Maggie as that of a "chanting priestess"; that of children as "no-necked monsters"; that of Big Daddy as a "bellowing bull"; that of Big Mama as a "huffing, puffing, old bulldog." Only Brick is described as genuine "music" in the confusion of noises. The playwright characterizes the House of Pollitt as "a great aviary of chattering birds." In a later work, *Orpheus Descending,* the playwright provides an even more elaborate sound score in which the major instrumentation is given to the Orphic guitar. Around this sound—the magical music of Orpheus, the dark god—the playwright weaves aural images of the dead: the sounds of hounds baying, death cries, and inarticulate prophetic portents. Such an image warns the audience of the approaching death of the protagonist:

[*The* NEGRO *nods, then throws back his turkey neck and utters a series of sharp barking sounds that rise to a sustained cry of great intensity and wildness. The cry produces a violent reaction in the building.* BEULAH *and* DOLLY *run out of the store.* LADY *does not move but she catches her breath.* DOG *and* PEE WEE *run down the stairs with ad libs and hustle the* NEGRO *out of the store, ignoring* LADY, *as their wives call:* 'PEE WEE!' *and* 'DAWG!' *outside on the walk.* VAL *sweeps back the alcove curtain and appears as if the cry were his cue. Above, in the sick room, hoarse, outraged shouts that subside with exhaustion. . . .*]

(Act III, Scene 3, pp. 102–3)

Williams has developed for the explication of his text an

entire grammar, a complex system of signs—a kind of iconography—for modern American theatre. This sensuous symbolic language is indebted, in part, to the theory and practice of Richard Wagner, Adolphe Appia, Gordon Craig, Erwin Piscator, and Bertolt Brecht. But Williams—like other contemporary American artists—has attempted to clothe his forms with contents which are distinctly American in origin and which are popular both in language and meaning.

As late as 1953, Williams believed that the measure of his accomplishment in the creation of an appropriate symbolic language was the play *Camino Real*.[7] He defined this drama as his "conception of the time and world in which he lived," and described its characters as "archetypes of basic attitudes and qualities" of people in that world. The essential idea of form here, as in earlier plays, is poetic vision—in this case, the vision of a humanity condemned to spiritual death in a walled city known as the "Camino Real." It is illuminating to compare the different levels of plasticity which are to be seen in the two published versions of this play (1948 and 1953). The first, *Ten Blocks on the Camino Real,* is a short play which appeared in the series *American Blues*. This play was apparently written some five years or more before the completion of the longer work, *Camino Real*. The early drama is an excellent example of Williams' early lyric form. In *Ten Blocks on the Camino Real* Williams divides his poetic vision into discrete units called "blocks," "stations" on the highway to human annihilation. These "blocks" are interpreted primarily as lyric figures, that is, as visual and aural images.

This first play employs speech sparingly; in addition to his general use of musical and choreographic movement, the playwright allows the action to crystallize, at given points, in elaborate spectacles. For example, the "streetcleaners" who appear periodically take the identity of "grotesques" borrowed from

7. Preface to *Camino Real,* p. ix.

medieval prints depicting the "Dance of Death." In Block VI, the Gypsy's daughter dances a flamenco in a general stage celebration. In the final scene, the playwright gives the following instructions for a short ballet:

The Fiesta DANCERS *enter. They are all in ghostly white costumes and their faces covered with neo-classic white masks. A spectral ballet is performed to the eerie music.* (Block X, p. 74)

In this short work, the lines of demarcation between music, speech, gesture, and dance have been, for all practical purposes, effaced.

In his subsequent development of this play Williams retains this primary level of lyric interpretation, but he expands the ideational content through the creation of additional levels of dramatic action. He develops his fragmentary story line by placing the dance drama within a framing structure, by ascribing the entire vision to the dreaming mind of a choral figure —Don Quixote. In order to interpret the dream, he employs a rigidly schematic arrangement of characters, a pattern of "ideographs" drawn from literary history. He describes this procession of character symbols as a "shadow play." Through these "shadows"—shaped from Western intellectual experiences— the playwright suggests, rather than explains, an idea about the nature of the world in which he lives. As these images —Quixote, Byron, Marguerite Gautier, Casanova, Kilroy, and others—appear in his "dream of time," they signify something more than personal lyricism; for they are the evidence of an effort to project a dynamic, plastic image of modern consciousness. Williams believes that in this drama he has achieved "plasticity"; that is to say, the later work, *Camino Real,* approaches the "synthesis" which is his ideal theatre.

The translation of this complex and abstract form into concrete language has required an elaborate instrumentation, manipulated by artists of broad theoretical knowledge and great talent. Williams has been extremely fortunate in having the services of many such artists at his disposal. Indeed, he has perhaps been the most fortunate of the American playwrights in this regard. His first work, *The Glass Menagerie,* was staged by one of the most gifted of American directors, Margo Jones. It was also Miss Jones who directed the first New York production of *Summer and Smoke,* a play which had been previewed in her own Dallas theatre. In his middle period Williams had the distinguished director Elia Kazan as the chief interpreter of his works. The creative relationship of Kazan to a larger group of technicians, actors, writers, and theorists is extremely important, not only to the development of Williams but to the entire history of contemporary American theatre. Since 1955, Williams' work has found expression at the hands of other artists, including Harold Clurman, José Quintero, Herbert Machiz, George Roy Hill, and Frank Corsaro.

The development of an appropriate instrumentation for Williams' plastic theatre is the culmination of a complex pattern of growth. Williams' theatre has emerged in part out of the activity of the American university. It has been in the classrooms of such men as George P. Baker, Brander Matthews, Kenneth Macgowan, and Thomas Dickinson that the American form has assumed its theoretical shape. Moreover, Williams is indebted for the technical principles of his dramaturgy to an extended period of experimentation in allied arts. The "plastic form" is a descendant in the hereditary line of dance theatre: of Isadora Duncan, Ruth St. Denis, Martha Graham, and Hanya Holm. Similarly, it is an heir to the achievement of the great cinematic directors, D. W. Griffith, Cecil B. DeMille, and Kazan himself. It owes some aspects of its shape to the tradition of American letters, especially to writers such as Whitman, Hawthorne, Poe, Melville, and Faulkner. Williams' idea of a plastic form is perhaps most clearly indebted to the experimentation of theatre groups which have, in the twentieth century, refined the techniques of the American arts of acting, staging, and design.

The collaboration of Williams, Kazan, Jo Mielziner, Lee

Strasberg, and, on occasion, Jean Rosenthal follows the precedent of Eugene O'Neill, George Cram Cook, Edna St. Vincent Millay, Kenneth Macgowan, Robert Edmond Jones, and Cleon Throckmorton at the Provincetown Playhouse between 1919 and 1929.[8] The plastic form of Tennessee Williams is a development made possible by the experimentation of these earlier artists, who created a rudimentary dramaturgy for the theatre of O'Neill. Plays such as *The Emperor Jones* and *The Hairy Ape* established precedents which Williams and his interpreters have continued to follow. O'Neill and his artistic collaborators made major strides, not only toward the evolution of a dramaturgy subject to a single aesthetic will, but also toward the creation of the kind of synthetic symbol which Williams and his interpreters have continued to develop.

Undoubtedly the most influential artist associated with the re-creation of Williams' texts on the stage is the distinguished director Elia Kazan. Indeed, it has been Kazan who has refined the production method associated with Williams' dramatic texts. Originally a member of the Group Theatre, Kazan was grounded in the "psychological naturalism" of this neo-Stanislavskian school. However, it is clear that this technique provided only a technical basis for his "American method." For like Williams himself, Kazan has so distilled and formalized the patterns of his "method" that he has arrived at a dramaturgy not unlike that of orthodox expressionists; that is, Kazan and his associates—particularly Jo Mielziner—have succeeded in abstracting from American realism-naturalism its formal essentials. It is important to recognize, then, that the plastic theatre of Williams, Kazan, and Mielziner is not a realistic form either in theory or in practice. On the contrary, it is a highly abstract kind, so effective in its use of a singular iconography that it appears to many spectators to copy reality.

An extremely important document in this connection is the personal notebook of Elia Kazan for the production of *A*

8. See Kenneth Macgowan, *The Theatre of Tomorrow* (New York, 1921).

Streetcar Named Desire.[9] These notes, originally published by Toby Cole and Helen Krich Chinoy, show the method of this director in formulating a set of correlatives for the shapes of Williams' imagination. Kazan describes *A Streetcar Named Desire* as "poetic tragedy." He echoes Williams' own language in his formulation of the theme:

Theme—this is a message from the dark interior. This little twisted, pathetic, confused bit of light and culture puts out a cry. It is snuffed out by the crude forces of violence, insensibility and vulgarity which exist in our South—and this cry is the play.

(*Directing the Play,* p. 296)

Like Williams, the director rejects "realist" methodology:

Style—one reason a "style," a stylized production is necessary is that a subjective factor—Blanche's memories, inner life, emotions, are a real factor. We cannot really understand her behavior unless we see the effect of her past on her present behavior. (Page 296)

He defines the key problem in the creation of a theoretical language for this play:

The style—the real deep style—consists of one thing only: to find behavior that's truly social, significantly typical, at each moment. . . .

And for the other characters, too, you face the same problem. To find the Don Quixote character for them. *This is a poetic tragedy, not a realistic or a naturalistic one. So you must find a Don Quixote scheme of things for each.* (Pages 297–98)

The director analyzes the central character in terms which are consistent with the playwright's description:

Her problem has to do with her tradition. Her notion of what a woman should be. She is stuck with this "ideal." It is her. It is her ego. Unless she lives by it, she cannot live; in fact her whole life has been for nothing. Even the Alan Gray incident as she now tells it and believes it to have been, is a necessary piece of romanticism. Essentially, in outline, she tells what happened, but it also serves the demands of her notion of

9. Elia Kazan, "Notebook for *A Streetcar Named Desire,*" in *Directing the Play,* eds. Toby Cole and Helen Krich Chinoy (Indianapolis, 1953), pp. 296–310.

herself, to make her *special* and different, out of the tradition of the romantic ladies of the past: Swinburne, Wm. Morris, Pre-Raphaelites, etc. This way it serves as an excuse for a great deal of her behavior.

Because this image of herself cannot be accomplished in reality, certainly not in the South of our day and time, it is her effort and practice to *accomplish it in fantasy.* Everything that she does in *reality* too is colored by this necessity, this compulsion to be *special.* So, in fact, *reality becomes fantasy* too. She makes it so! (Pages 298–99)

Kazan seeks a method of giving concrete shape to Williams' idea of character:

The variety essential to the play, and to Blanche's playing and to Jessica Tandy's achieving the role demands that she be a "heavy" at the beginning. For instance: contemplate the inner character contradiction: bossy yet helpless, domineering yet shaky, etc. The audience at the beginning should see her bad effect on Stella, want Stanley to tell her off. He does. He exposes her and then gradually, as they see how genuinely in pain, how actually desperate she is . . . then they begin to go with her. They begin to realize that they are sitting in at the death of something extraordinary . . . colorful, varied, passionate, lost, witty, imaginative, of her own integrity . . . and then they feel the tragedy.

. . . .

Try to find an entirely different character, a self-dramatized and self-romanticized character for Blanche to play in each scene. She is playing 11 different people. This will give it a kind of changeable and shimmering surface it should have. And all these 11 self-dramatized and romantic characters should be out of the romantic tradition of the Pre-Bellum South, etc. Example: Sc. 2 Gay Miss Devil-may-care.

(Pages 299–300)

The director prepares a method for the transposition of the written drama into concrete images. He describes his key image in these terms:

Blanche is a butterfly in a jungle looking for just a little momentary protection, doomed to a sudden, early violent death. The more I work on Blanche, incidentally, the less insane she seems. She is caught in a fatal inner contradiction, but in another society, she *would* work. In Stanley's society, no!

This is like a classic tragedy. Blanche is Medea or someone pursued by the Harpies, the Harpies being *her own nature.* Her inner sickness pursues her like *doom* and makes it impossible for her to attain the one thing she needs: a safe harbor. (Page 301)

Kazan makes his own analysis of the eleven images of the play:

1. Blanche comes to the last stop at the end of the line.
2. Blanche tries to make a place for herself.
3. Blanche breaks them apart, but when they come together, Blanche is more alone than ever!
4. Blanche, more desperate because more excluded, tries the direct attack and makes the enemy who will finish her.
5. Blanche finds that she is being tracked down for the kill. She must work fast.
6. Blanche suddenly finds, suddenly makes for herself, the only possible, perfect man for her.
7. Blanche comes out of the happy bathroom to find that her own doom has caught up with her.
8. Blanche fights her last fight. Breaks down. Even Stella deserts her.
9. Blanche's last desperate effort to save herself by telling the whole truth. The *truth dooms her.*
10. Blanche escapes out of this world. She is brought back by Stanley and destroyed.
11. Blanche is disposed of. (Page 297)

In these analyses—written for himself—Kazan demonstrates his technique in developing a subordinate system of plastic symbols, a linguistic scheme for the explication of the text. Kazan's symbols are concrete; that is, his language represents the effective transliteration of Williams' text into acting, staging patterns, music, sound effects, and scenic design. Kazan's notes illustrate the importance of the interpretative artist in the plastic theatre of Williams. For if the idea of plastic theatre has been formulated by Williams, it has remained for secondary artists to give to this idea its sensible form.

Design, word, gesture, mime, music, dance, and light in the drama of Tennessee Williams are components of a sensuous symbol. The recovery of this comprehensive dramatic motive in the theatre of the twentieth century has necessitated changes in the nature of theatrical representation. Williams has moved away from the concrete interests of the realists, and beyond the essentially lyric concerns of the romantics, to a language which strives to effect a reconciliation of all facets of reality. The dramaturgic form which this playwright has developed is indebted to the romantic theorists—particularly to Wagner and Appia—for its conception of the interpretative symbol. But it is important to observe that the use of symbols in the theatre of Williams differs from those conceived by earlier artists and theorists. For the contemporary theatre, as Fergusson points out, is not primarily concerned with "art for art's sake," but rather with the creation of a drama which can rediscover—or create—comprehensive universal meanings. Music, dance, mime, poetry, and design are not, in the theatre of Williams, techniques employed for the unadorned delight of the spectator. They are philosophical—even theological—in their intent, for they attempt to re-establish the ritual function of theatre. They are intended as modes of signification: signs of a present search for truth.

chapter six

CAMINO REAL: THE WORLD AS SPECTACLE

The world is my idea.

The preceding chapters have attempted to define those concepts that have determined the idea of form in the drama of Tennessee Williams. The evidence of the plays seems to support the conclusion that Williams' form is poetic in its intent: that he seeks to confront contemporary man with an image of his condition. This motive has produced in the theatre of Williams a change from traditional practices affecting (1) the concept of dramatic action, (2) the construct of myth, (3) the nature of the protagonist, and (4) the shape of the production form. In the course of his development, the playwright has built complex patterns of myth, created new symbolic struc-

NOTE TO CHAPTER TITLE: In suggesting that history may be reduced to a procession of images—a spectacle arising from his own consciousness—Williams

tures, and evolved a distinctive image of man. His contemporary form is, by description, a synthetic entity, derived from the union of diverse forms and techniques, borrowed in part from literature, the painting arts, cinema, and the dance. Like these related forms, the drama of Williams reflects a sensibility peculiar to the age.

From the point of view of the student of American drama, perhaps the best example of the form of Tennessee Williams is *Camino Real* (1953); for this work demonstrates clearly the primary characteristics that identify Williams' idea of theatre. So different is *Camino Real* from traditional kinds of drama that some critics have described it by invented names such as "anti-drama," "comic-tragedy," "anti-theatre," and "grotesque mime." The American critic Eric Bentley describes this extended kind—the form of *Camino Real*—as "magic theatre," drama which seeks to be more than theatre.[1] Certainly, in *Camino Real* Williams makes a definite break with the realist tradition, a departure more calculated than that of *The Glass Menagerie* and even more radical than that exemplified in *Summer and Smoke*. The important fact, however, is that *Camino Real* established Williams not only as a popular dramatist but as an artist whose idea of form is derived in part from recent developments in philosophy, theology, and politics, as well as in dance, cinema, literature, and the plastic arts.

Camino Real, like other examples of Williams' work, illustrates the necessity for a new definition of form. Clearly, neither the Aristotelian definition, the Horatian imperative, the romantic concept, nor the realist law provides a satisfactory basis for judging such a play. *Camino Real* is not "drama" in the sense prescribed by previous laws. Measured by older concepts, it

---

employs an idea similar to one articulated by Arthur Schopenhauer. Schopenhauer, also concerned with giving concrete representation to the progression of conscious experience, described the world as "Will and Idea." See *The World as Will and Idea,* trans. R. B. Haldane and J. Kemp (London, 1896), pp. 3–6. The epigraph is from Schopenhauer's work.

1. Eric Bentley, *In Search of Theater* (New York, 1953), pp. 360–69.

may be described as "tableau," "lyric," "poetry," or "dance." It is, in the ancient language of Horace, the image of "a sick man's dreams, so that neither head nor foot can be assigned to a single shape." [2] Williams would no doubt agree with Horace, but would suggest that the "sick man" of his description is humanity.

The authority for this choice of a work for close analysis is the playwright himself. In 1953 Williams wrote that he had given more attention to the problem of internal and external design in *Camino Real* than in any other work. The quotation, although given on page 36, bears repeating at this point.

> My desire was to give these audiences my own sense of something wild and unrestricted that ran like water in the mountains, or clouds changing shape in a gale, or the continually dissolving and transforming images of a dream. This sort of freedom is not chaos nor anarchy. On the contrary, it is the result of painstaking design, and in this work I have given more conscious attention to form and construction than I have in any work before. . . . (Foreword, p. ix)

Previous discussions of Williams' idea of form have indicated that the playwright conceives of his drama as the concretion of vision. In order to give sensible shape to poetic insight, he has attempted to evolve an objective language—a system of concrete symbols for his plastic form. *Camino Real* is articulated in such a language. Williams describes this play as a progression, as a moving chain of plastic images. In his effort to transpose this dynamic form to the stage, the dramatist has assumed the prerogatives of a painter, a sculptor, or a composer. Again the words of Horace are relevant: "Painters and poets,' you say, 'have always had an equal right in hazarding anything.' " [3] For *Camino Real,* the instrumentation of the drama is not merely words. The play is articulated in the synthetic language of the plastic theatre: in gesture, sound, music, dance, light, color, action, and design. ". . . But I think of writing as something

2. Horace *The Art of Poetry,* trans. H. Rushton Fairclough in *Horace* (London, 1926), p. 451.

3. *Loc. cit.*

more organic than words, something closer to being and action. I want to work more and more with a more plastic theatre than the one I have [worked with] before."[4]

The written play is, in the language of Williams, only the score: "And in my dissident opinion, a play in a book is only the shadow of a play and not even a clear shadow of it. . . . The printed script of a play is hardly more than an architect's blueprint of a house not yet built or built and destroyed."[5] For Tennessee Williams as for Adolphe Appia, drama, like music, is an ineffable substance whose existence is only symbolized on the page: "The score is set down on paper, just like the manuscripts of the dramatist; the conventional symbols of music are the equivalent of those other conventional symbols, the letters of the alphabet; and the presence of the composer is the same human presence as that of the dramatist. Where, then, lies the difference?"[6]

If the text of this play serves as its score, Williams uses, as its co-ordinating motif, rhythm. The drama thus follows a principle set out by James Joyce in *A Portrait of the Artist as a Young Man.* "Rhythm—said Stephen—is the first formal esthetic relation of part to part in any esthetic whole or of an esthetic whole to its part or parts or of any part to the esthetic whole of which it is a part."[7] *Camino Real* seems to illustrate more than does any other work created by Williams his concept of plastic form, of multidimensional design in motion.

Camino Real began life as a short sketch, as a poetic piece for actor-dancer-musicians. The title of the early lyric drama, published in 1948, was *Ten Blocks on the Camino Real.* The Broad-

4. Preface to *Cat on a Hot Tin Roof,* p. viii.
5. Preface to *Camino Real,* p. xii.
6. Adolphe Appia, "The Future of Production" (*Theater Arts Anthology,* eds. Rosamond Gilder and others [New York, 1950]), p. 521.
7. James Joyce, *A Portrait of the Artist as a Young Man* (London: Egoist Press, 1916), p. 241.

way version, *Camino Real,* staged by Elia Kazan in 1953, was, according to the author, the result of a major revision in which the director took an active part:

> Elia Kazan was attracted to this work mainly, I believe, for the same reason—its freedom and mobility of form. I know that we have kept saying the word "flight" to each other as if the play were merely an abstraction of the impulse to fly, and most of the work out of town, his in staging, mine in cutting and revising, has been with this impulse in mind: the achievement of a continual flow. Speech after speech and bit after bit that were nice in themselves have been remorselessly blasted out of the script and its staging wherever they seemed to obstruct or divert this flow. (Foreword, p. ix)

The final version of the drama, according to the Editor's note (Preface, p. xiv), was the result of still more extensive reshaping: "Three characters, a prologue and several scenes that were not in the Broadway production have been added, or reinstated from earlier, preproduction versions, while other scenes have been deleted."

The comprehensive reorganization of this play, a process which may not yet be finished, would seem to indicate that a discrepancy existed between the vision of the artist and the realization of that poetic moment. For this reason, it is enlightening to compare the fundamental differences between these stages in the creative process, to examine both phases of the author's development toward a mature mode of expression. It is important to note that the basic construct of both published versions of the *Camino Real* is that of vision: poetic revelation. Williams' vision in this drama is theological, even apocalyptic. Like Strindberg, William Blake, Dante, or St. John, he foresees the end of humanity, a humanity condemned to spiritual death:

> I know this place. . . . Here it is on the chart. Look, it says here: "Continue until you come to the square of a walled town which is the end of the Ca*mi*no Re*al* and the beginning of the *Ca*mino *Re*al. Halt there," it says, "and turn back, Traveler, for the spring of humanity has gone dry in this place and—" (*Camino Real,* Prologue, p. 5)

This vision of a dying world is the internal form of the *Camino Real.*

Like Sartre in *The Flies,* Cocteau in *The Infernal Machine,* and Wilder in *The Skin of Our Teeth,* Williams attempted, first, to realize his vision through symbol. *Camino Real,* by traditional definition, is a kind of allegory, a twentieth-century parable. In the early play, the dramatist projects his moral fable in purely poetic symbols. *Ten Blocks on the Camino Real* is a kind of lyric play for dancers. The preliminary directions include this description:

> As the curtain rises there are stationary figures about the plaza. These figures will be variously used as vendors, dancers and chorus of the "Laboratory" scene. A group of ten dancers would suffice for all chorus uses. They are crouching, leaning and lying about the plaza in their dust-colored rags. . . . One of the street-figures is distinct from the others. She is an ancient woman who wears a snow-white rebozo and who is vending those glittering and gaudy flowers made of tin that are used at peasant funerals in the Latin Americas. Her voice is softer and more musical than the others, and her face remains hidden by the blanket until the "Laboratory" scene when she becomes La Madrecita de las Soledadas. . . .
>
> Also distinct from the others is a guitar player whose instrument is blue: he is dressed as a Mexican street-musician, though he may wear a domino to indicate he is somewhat outside the play, being a sort of master of ceremonies. The guitar and singing may be used at more points than are indicated in the script: the same is true of dancing; though it should not impede a lively progress of scenes. . . .
>
> (*Ten Blocks . . . ,* Stage Directions, p. 44)

The first play, then, is an allegory which is projected as a pattern of images, symbols barely elaborated by exposition. In this play there are ten such figures, some almost bare of discursive explication. The burden of communication rests on the playwright's iconographical system: on dance, mime, and the total design of all theatrical elements. Many details of Williams' iconography may be described as "Gothic." His symbolism here is closely related to that of medieval liturgy, as well as to that popular form, the *commedia dell' arte*—itself a kind of symbolic theatre. *Ten Blocks on the Camino Real* is a kind of pageant: a mime of the spectacle of existence. In it Williams recalls the religious processions of the Middle Ages, the pageantry of the miracle plays, as well as the profane and near-sacriligious mimicry of festival days. Many of the images of *Camino Real* are grotesques, drawn from the plastic arts; in this early version of the play, the following description is given the Death Mummers:

(The STREETCLEANERS *enter through arch at top of alley and advance into plaza, trundling their big white barrel on wheels, old German prints of the "Dance of Death" will suggest their appearance, except that they wear white jackets and caps and have brooms. . . .)*

(*Ten Blocks* . . . , Block IV, p. 52)

The playwright develops these figures more fully in the second version of this drama:

[*A Hunchback Mummer somersaults through his hoop of silver bells, springs up and shakes it excitedly toward a downstage arch which begins to flicker with a diamond-blue radiance; this marks the advent of each legendary character in the play. . . .*] (*Camino Real,* Block VII, p. 58)

. . . [*W*]*eird-looking celebrants or carnival mummers creep into the plaza, silently as spiders descending a wall.*

(*Camino Real,* Block X, p. 99)

In his early play, then, Williams creates from the components of many forms a kind of ironic vision. *Ten Blocks on the Camino Real* is a dumb show, a bitter charade, which mirrors the triumph of evil over good, and which reveals the interchangeability of death and life, the tragic and the comic. Its metamorphic figures, like the Sphinx of Cocteau, appear, disappear, and reappear; they unroll, divide, extend, contract, and merge in a manner which is essentially demonic.[8] In this grotesque mime, the penetration of the world as spectacle, Williams

8. Jean Cocteau, *La Machine Infernale* (Paris: Editions Bernard Grasset, 1934), pp. 117–18.

seeks to decipher the same enigmatic problem which has occupied his attention in all of his works: the problem of meaning and intelligibility in human experience.

The progress from *Ten Blocks on the Camino Real* to the later version, *Camino Real,* repeats a general pattern of complication in theme and form which may be observed elsewhere in Williams' work. *Camino Real* differs from *Ten Blocks on the Camino Real* in its more mature symbolic development and in the addition of a second and perhaps even a third level of explication. Williams begins the second version by declaring that his intent is the exposure of value systems. Like Sartre, he not only attempts to expose false values, he attacks what he considers to be comprehensive forms of immorality in the world of the twentieth century. The dramatist reveals in this work a highly developed ethical concept—a system of valuation which reflects many correspondences to the theories of existential philosophers such as Sartre and Karl Jaspers.[9] For it is clear in *Camino Real* that Williams interprets the human dilemma in our time as the result of an extended moral crisis. He opens this play with the search of a world-weary "Don Quixote" for a man of honor in contemporary life:

> QUIXOTE: It also reminds an old knight of that green country he lived in which was the youth of his heart, before such singing words as *Truth!*
>
> SANCHO [*panting*]:—Truth!
>
> QUIXOTE: *Valor!*
>
> SANCHO: —Valor.
>
> QUIXOTE [*elevating his lance*]: *Devoir!*
>
> SANCHO:—Devoir. . .
>
> QUIXOTE:—turned into the meaningless mumble of some old monk hunched over cold mutton at supper!
>
> (*Camino Real,* Prologue, pp. 3–4)

Transgression on the Camino Real is interpreted, initially, as the loss of honor:

9. Karl Jaspers, *Reason and Existenz,* trans. William Earle (New York, 1955).

"Leave with honor?" Your vocabulary is almost as out-of-date as your cape and your cane. How could anyone quit this field with honor, this place where there's nothing but the gradual wasting away of everything decent in us . . . the sort of desperation that comes after even desperation has been worn out through long wear! . . . Why have they put these screens around the table? (*Camino Real,* Block VII, p. 72)

This absence of honor is illustrated in regard to each of the major figures in the plaza. Significantly, it is the sin of the poet Byron:

—That was my vocation once upon a time, before it was obscured by vulgar plaudits!—Little by little it was lost among gondolas and palazzos!—masked balls, glittering salons, huge shadowy courts and torch-lit entrances! . . .

. . . .

. . . *There is a passion for declivity in this world!*

And lately I've found myself listening to hired musicians behind a row of artificial palm trees—instead of the single—pure-stringed instrument of my heart. . . . (Block VIII, pp. 77–78)

Williams concludes his play with a prayer for the return of honor to the world: ". . . Oh, sometime and somewhere, let there be something to mean the word *honor* again."[10]

Williams illustrates the destruction of moral values in contemporary life by holding up to scrutiny the traditional romantic themes: love, power, success, and death. He shows the disintegration of each of these poetic ideals in a way which distinguishes his contemporary perspective from that of the orthodox romantics. For the progression on the Camino Real records the disintegration of such ideals; its use of them is, like its visual tone, ironic. One of the rapidly disintegrating values on the Camino Real is respect for the individual:

Now you want to know what is done to a body from which the soul has departed on the Camino Real!—Its disposition depends on what the Streetcleaners happen to find in its pockets. If its pockets are empty as the unfortunate Baron's turned out to be, and as mine are at this moment—the "stiff" is wheeled straight off to the Laboratory. And there the individual becomes an undistinguished member of a collectivist state.

10. Block XVI, p. 156.

His chemical components are separated and poured into vats containing the corresponding elements of countless others. If any of his vital organs or parts are at all unique in size or structure, they're placed on exhibition in bottles containing a very foul-smelling solution called formaldehyde. There is a charge of admission to this museum. The proceeds go to the maintenance of the military police. (Block V, pp. 42–43)

A second value which the playwright describes as a "lost cause" is human compassion:

THE DREAMER: *Hermano!*

. . . .

GUTMAN [*to the waiter*]: *Put up the ropes!*
The word was spoken. The crowd is agitated. Hang on!

JACQUES [*hoarsely, shaken*]: He said "Hermano." That's the word for brother.

GUTMAN [*calmly*]: Yes, the most dangerous word in any human tongue is the word for brother. It's inflammatory.—I don't suppose it can be struck out of the language altogether but it must be reserved for strictly private usage in back of soundproof walls. Otherwise it disturbs the population . . .

JACQUES: The people need the word. They're thirsty for it!

GUTMAN: What are these creatures? Mendicants. Prostitutes. Thieves and petty vendors in a bazaar where the human heart is a part of the bargain.

JACQUES: Because they need the word and the word is forbidden!

GUTMAN: The word is said in pulpits and at tables of council where its volatile essence can be contained. But on the lips of these creatures, what is it? A wanton excitement to riot, without understanding. For what is a brother to them but someone to get ahead of, to cheat, to lie to, to undersell in the market. Brother, you say to a man whose wife you sleep with!— (Block II, pp. 20–22)

Perhaps the most ironically treated of the romantic themes is that of death. Death on the plaza is not the symbol of finality and grandeur that it is in romantic literature. On the Camino Real, death, like life, is an absurdity. Williams describes the death of a man in these ironic terms:

[*The Survivor stumbles forward. The Officer fires at him. He lowers his hands to his stomach, turns slowly about with a lost expression, looking up at the sky, and stumbles toward the fountain. During the scene that follows, until the entrance of La Madrecita and her Son, the*

Survivor drags himself slowly about the concrete rim of the fountain, almost entirely ignored, as a dying pariah dog in a starving country. . . .]

. . . .

[*The Survivor has come out upon the forestage, now, not like a dying man but like a shy speaker who has forgotten the opening line of his speech. He is only a little crouched over with a hand obscuring the red stain over his belly. Two or three Street People wander about calling their wares. . . . The Survivor arrives at the top of the stairs descending into the orchestra of the theatre, and hangs onto it, looking out reflectively as a man over the rail of a boat coming into a somewhat disturbingly strange harbor.*] (Block II, pp. 14–15)

Death on the Camino Real is a grotesque gesture, a sly joke. Williams re-creates the sensibility of Hamlet's gravediggers in his Streetcleaners, who take away the dying in garbage cans:

[*There is the sound of the Streetcleaners' piping. They trundle their white barrel into the plaza from one of the downstage arches. The appearance of these men undergoes a progressive alteration through the play. When they first appear they are almost like any such public servants in a tropical country; their white jackets are dirtier than the musicians' and some of the stains are red. They have on white caps with black visors. They are continually exchanging sly jokes and giggling unpleasantly together. . . .*] (Block III, p. 30)

This ghostly procession of diminished values makes of this play more than a charade, a progression of images in a plastic medium. *Camino Real,* like Claudel's *The Satin Slipper,* Wilder's *The Skin of Our Teeth,* Sartre's *The Flies,* and Anouilh's *Antigone,* is a kind of "thesis play." Williams attempts to bring into focus on the Camino Real new implications affecting the present condition of man. He interprets the contemporary epoch as a time of acute crisis, as a juncture in history where the fate of man again hangs in the balance. *Camino Real* is a mythic projection of a moment of decision which engages mankind in the mid-twentieth century. The playwright attempts to explore, with the aid of his synthetic myth, all of the possibilities contingent on this fateful moment in human destiny.

Williams reviews Western history through a literary "glass." There passes across the sight of the spectator "the world as spectacle," a "panorama of lost legends." He recalls to time Marguerite Gautier, the "Lady of the Camellias"; Jacques Casanova, the "great lover"; Lord Byron, the poet; Baron de Charlus, the decadent aristocrat; and Lord Mulligan, a tycoon of the twentieth century. Each of these figures symbolizes an era of modern Western history—a world view:

> Ah, there's the music of another legend, one that everyone knows, the legend of the sentimental whore, the courtesan who made the mistake of love. But now you see her coming into this plaza not as she was when she burned with a fever that cast a thin light over Paris, but changed, yes, faded as lanterns and legends fade when they burn into day! (Block VII, pp. 58–59)

With the movement of these characters across the stage, Williams projects the "rise and fall of heroes," the passage of time and history in theatrical abstraction.

Williams describes each of these figures—and the epochs they represent—as having lost in "the game of being against non-being." The persistently unsolved problems of humanity are articulated by Marguerite Gautier:

> What are we sure of? Not even of our existence, dear comforting friend! And whom can we ask the questions that torment us? "What is this place?" "Where are we?"—a fat old man who gives sly hints that only bewilder us more, a fake of a Gypsy squinting at cards and tea-leaves. What else are we offered? The never-broken procession of little events that assure us that we and strangers about us are still going on! Where? Why? and the perch that we hold is unstable! We're threatened with eviction, for this is a port of entry and departure, there are no permanent guests! And where else have we to go when we leave here? Bide-a-while? "Ritz Men Only?" Or under that ominous arch into Terra Incognita? We're lonely. We're frightened. We hear the Streetcleaners' piping not far away. . . . (Block X, p. 96)

Williams is clearly concerned in this play with the ultimate questions of being, meaning, and action. He attempts to interpret the enigma of human experience in a way particularly relevant to our time.

Because of the questions which it poses, some critics regard the major interest of this work as philosophical, even theological, in nature. The Bochum critics describe *Camino Real* as a theological vision, as a contemporary rendition of Dante's *Divine Comedy:*

In order to understand *Camino Real* completely, one needs a "Baedeker." The beginnings compare: Wayward persons come to this unusual place where things happen intolerably and where every man tortures the other, where an eternal complaining and groaning, pressing and pounding, rules. This puzzling locality is described precisely in Dante: it is that middle realm between life and death where at the end of their life's journey all men gather. They are already dead but still have not lost their memory of earthly life; this memory burdens and pains them yet; they always want to go back again, while the way back is barred.[11]

Williams, these critics point out, fashions a contemporary Inferno based on legends out of Western literary traditions:

The title is consciously supposed to enclose an ambiguity. If one expresses "Camino Real" in English, that means "the way of reality." If one expresses it in Spanish, then it means "Royal Road". . . . In this double meaning already lies hidden what Tennessee Williams wants to say . . . the road of the Spanish knights who conquered the land, but also the road upon which Christianity came to the West Coast of America. This, moreover, is the division of the play into sixteen stations also explained —the missionary stations . . . lay upon this way, a day's journey from one another. . . . Today, however, the old missionary way has become a street of industry, of money, of tourist trade—a business reality.[12]

The playwright had, however, other models for his Inferno, such cities as became familiar in the headlines during World War II. The actual highways after which the author has fashioned his road to death saw thousands of refugees vainly fleeing from persecution into a "place of intolerable transition between life and death."

Camino Real represents such a road from life to death; its blocks are "stations of the cross" in man's progression toward

11. *Bochumer Diskussion über "Camino Real" von Tennessee Williams* (Frankfurt-am-Main, 1955), p. 8.

12. *Op. cit.*, pp. 5–6.

annihilation. The "plaza," the last of these way stations, may be described as an "absurd universe" for there appears no cohesive force within it. It is merely a place of entry and departure, "with no permanent guests" (Block VIII, p. 73). Its ambiguous host, Gutman, defines the nature of human existence on the Camino Real:

> —They suffer from extreme fatigue, our guests at the Siete Mares, all of them have a degree or two of fever. Questions are passed amongst them like something illicit and shameful, like counterfeit money or drugs or indecent postcards—
>
> . . . .
>
> My guests are confused and exhausted but at this hour they pull themselves together, and drift downstairs on the wings of gin and the lift, they drift into the public rooms and exchange notes again on fashionable couturiers and custom tailors, restaurants, vintages of wine, hair-dressers, plastic surgeons, girls and young men susceptible to offers. . .
>
> (Block II, pp. 15–16)

Gutman comments on the universality of anxiety and despair on the Camino Real:

> When the big wheels crack on this street, it's like the fall of a capital city, the destruction of Carthage, the sack of Rome by the white-eyed giants from the North! . . . I've seen the destruction of them! Adventurers suddenly frightened of a dark room! Gamblers unable to choose between odd and even! Con men and pitchmen and plume-hatted cavaliers turned baby-soft at one note of the Streetcleaners' pipes! When I observe this change, I say to myself: "Could it happen to ME?"—The answer is "YES!" And that's what curdles my blood like milk on the doorstep of someone gone for the summer! (Block VII, p. 58)

People suffer on the Camino Real, as in other locations in Williams' universe, from intolerable fear and anxiety:

> Are you perplexed by something? Are you tired out and confused? Do you have a fever?
>
> Do you feel yourself to be spiritually unprepared for the age of exploding atoms? Do you distrust the newspapers? Are you suspicious of governments? Have you arrived at a point on the Camino Real where the walls converge not in the distance but right in front of your nose? Does further progress appear impossible to you? Are you afraid of anything at all? Afraid of your heartbeat? Or the eyes of strangers! Afraid

of breathing? Afraid of not breathing? Do you wish that things could be straight and simple again as they were in your childhood? Would you like to go back to Kindy Garten? (Block III, p. 28)

But if Camino Real is a contemporary Inferno, Williams describes the sins of its sufferers in the language of the streets. Like Cocteau in *The Infernal Machine,* he renders an ancient idea in a present idiom—in this case in the pseudo-poetry of film love scenes; in the jargon of advertising agencies; in the "hipster" talk of the "beat poets"; in the intimate tones of gossip columnists; in the technical language of social agencies; and in the official "tough talk" of guards and police. In *Camino Real,* Williams fashions a hell of contemporary definition out of the language of the common man:

[*. . . The scene gathers wild momentum, is punctuated by crashes of percussion. Grotesque mummers act as demon custom inspectors and immigration authorities, etc. Baggage is tossed about, ripped open, smuggled goods seized, arrests made, all amid the wildest importunities, protests, threats, bribes, entreaties; it is a scene for improvisation.*]
(Block IX, p. 85)

He creates a particularly contemporary image of human suffering and damnation. For on the Camino Real, as in Dante's *Inferno,* there is no real and present God. On the Camino Real, God is absent, whether by choice or necessity. Man is his own cause, his own reason; it is he who is responsible for his destruction.

But *Camino Real* is not only concerned with picturing transgression; like earlier morality plays it seeks to discover a mode of human salvation. Williams, the American, finds in the antiheroic Kilroy a possible savior of humanity. The dramatist's choice of this figure as an image of a virtuous man is significant. It would have seemed logical that Williams, the poet, might have chosen a more romantic figure as the ritual savior of mankind; indeed, he makes of Casanova and Marguerite near-heroes. But in subordinating these two figures to the "clown"

Kilroy, the playwright appears to reject his more familiar protagonists, the "weak and beautiful" figures of earlier dramas. Seemingly, the playwright rejects his romantic protagonists because of their moral weaknesses, and particularly because of their indifference to suffering. Marguerite Gautier confesses her capacity for self-seeking to Jacques:

> So now and then, although we've wounded each other time and again—we stretch out hands to each other in the dark that we can't escape from—we huddle together for some dim-communal comfort—and that's what passes for love on this terminal stretch of the road that used to be royal. (Block X, pp. 96–97)

In *Camino Real,* Williams' vision of the protagonist seems to have undergone major change. For he embodies in Kilroy more radical conditions of courage than those which appear in the protagonists of his earlier works. Kilroy, legendary G.I. of World War II, modern "Ulysses" in search of meaning in the unnamed ports of the world—former hero, lover, and conqueror —is an image of the absurd. Gutman welcomes his arrival:

> Ho, ho!—a clown! The Eternal Punchinella! That's exactly what's needed in a time of crisis! (Block II, p. 24)

In his construction of this protagonist, Williams projects an existential image of man. Like Sartre, he sees a humanity destined for ambiguous suffering, for comic and absurd anguish. In Kilroy he symbolizes mankind's capacity for absurd suffering in behalf of others as well as for himself: Kilroy is humanity "with a heart."

> Feel my chest! Go on, feel it! Feel it. I've got a heart in my chest as big as the head of a baby. Ha–ha!
> (*Ten Blocks on the Camino Real,* Block II, p. 46)

But Kilroy, unlike the Sartrean protagonist, has retained throughout his travail in life a sense of honor:

> These are my gloves, these gloves are gold, and I fought a lot of hard fights to win 'em! I broke clean from the clinches. I never hit a low blow, the referee never told me to mix it up! And the fixers never got to me. (*Camino Real,* Block IV, p. 37)

Most important to this play is the fact that Kilroy, unlike Sartrean man, has retained human compassion; he is able to signal the word "brother," even when it cannot be spoken, with the blinking of his comic nose.

Because he has these virtues—courage, honor, and sympathy—Kilroy is chosen as the "Patsy," as the anti-hero:

> GUTMAN: Here, Boy! Take these.
>
> [*Gutman displays and then tosses on the ground at Kilroy's feet the Patsy outfit—the red fright wig, the big crimson nose that lights up and has horned rimmed glasses attached, a pair of clown pants that have a huge footprint on the seat.*]
>
> KILROY: What is this outfit?
>
> GUTMAN: The uniform of a Patsy.
>
> KILROY: I know what a Patsy is—he's a clown in the circus who takes prat-falls but *I'm no Patsy!*
>
> GUTMAN: Pick it up.
>
> KILROY: Don't give me orders. Kilroy is a free agent—
>
> GUTMAN [*smoothly*]: But a Patsy isn't. Pick it up and put it on, Candy Man. You are now the Patsy. (Block VI, pp. 48–49)

Williams finds in Kilroy a protagonist possessing the anti-heroic virtues of courage, honor, and compassion. That the anti-heroic Kilroy is a clown, a "little man," is significant. For Williams presses the existentialist idea of man as actor to one of its logical conclusions: man the clown, "the absurd." But Williams goes beyond the position of orthodox existentialism by creating a protagonist who is capable of a "feeling" sympathy rather than a "reasoned" compassion. It is Kilroy's feeling which enables him to transcend anti-heroism with a new "heroism"—love. Kilroy arrives at heroism intuitively. Although he is chosen as the "Patsy" by an unnamed power over which he has no control, his courage is revealed in the way in which he meets his fate. Understandably, he begins by searching for an escape:

> How do I git out? Which way do I go, which way do I get out? Where's the Greyhound depot? Hey, do you know where the Greyhound bus depot is? What's the best way out, if there is any way out? I got to find one. I had enough of this place. I had too much of this place.

I'm free. I'm a free man with equal rights in this world! You better believe it because that's news for you and you had better believe it! Kilroy's a free man with equal rights in this world! All right, now, help me, somebody, help me find a way out, I got to find one, I don't like this place! It's not for me and I am not buying any! Oh! Over there! I see a sign that says EXIT. That's a sweet word to me, man, that's a lovely word, EXIT! That's the entrance to paradise for Kilroy! Exit, I'm coming, Exit, I'm coming! (Block VI, pp. 50–51)

Kilroy searches for an exit, an escape from the Streetcleaners. He misses "The Fugitivo," the Charon's Boat. He makes an unsuccessful attempt at salvation by falling in love with Esmeralda, the reincarnation of innocence. Finally, he is forced to face the terror of his situation, the sound of the "Streetcleaners" piping in the distance. Kilroy makes an affirmation of faith in humanity, in a demonstration of greater courage than Williams has been inclined to reflect in his earlier protagonists:

—Washed up!—Finished!

[*Piping.*]

. . . that ain't a word that a man can't look at . . . There ain't no words in the language a man can't look at . . . and know just what they mean, and be. And act. And *go!*

[*He turns to the waiting Streetcleaners.*]

Come on! . . . Come on! . . . COME ON, YOU SONS OF BITCHES! KILROY IS HERE! HE'S READY!

[*A gong sounds*]

[*Kilroy swings at the Streetcleaners. They circle about him out of reach, turning him by each of their movements. The swings grow wilder like a boxer. He falls to his knees still swinging and finally collapses flat on his face.*]

[*The Streetcleaners pounce, but La Madrecita throws herself protectingly over the body and covers it with her shawl.*]

(Block XIV, pp. 146–47)

In *Camino Real,* Tennessee Williams chronicles the ordeal of the common man in our time. He describes his suffering, the same anguish which the continental dramatists call "absurdity." But Williams interprets metaphysical "dread" in the language of the streets:

> Had for a button! Stewed, screwed and tattooed on the Camino Real! Baptized, finally, with the contents of a slop-jar!—Did anybody say the deal was rugged?! (Block XVI, p. 157)

When his protagonist is destroyed, Williams mourns him, the symbol of all "maimed creatures, deformed, mutilated and homeless" throughout the world. He creates, in the sixteenth block of *Camino Real,* a coda. Block Sixteen celebrates the resurrection of Kilroy, the "rise of the Phoenix"; it allows the dramatist to pose a possibility of hope for humanity. Williams prays for a humanity characterized by error:

> God bless all con men and hustlers and pitch-men who hawk their hearts on the street, all two-time losers who're likely to lose once more, the courtesan who made the mistake of love, the greatest of lovers crowned with the longest horns, the poet who wandered far from his heart's green country and possibly will and possibly won't be able to find his way back. . . . (Block XVI, pp. 155–56)

He asks blessings on those world-weary knights, Quixote and Kilroy, who face life with the vestiges of an assaulted honor:

> . . . [L]ook down with a smile tonight on the last cavaliers, the ones with the rusty armor and soiled white plumes, and visit with understanding and something that's almost tender those fading legends that come and go in this plaza like songs not clearly remembered. . . .
> (Block XVI, p. 156)

The fountain of humanity is set flowing again by Kilroy's honor, tenderness, and compassion; the "violets in the mountains" spring up again. Williams, in his exhortation to endurance with compassion and courage, appends an affirmation which is articulated in both Christian doctrine and existentialist dogma.

Camino Real, a vision of the destruction of the modern world, is a part of the shock literature designed, according to the Bochum critics, to challenge the kind of moral apathy characteristic of many segments of modern society. "Williams would like to say to Americans: your imagined security is false, your belief in this way of Camino Real, of money, is unreal—this world is not in order."[13] In this play Williams poses many of the critical questions which confront all mankind in the twentieth century. For these questions he does not appear to offer systematic answers. He seeks, rather, to have the spectator examine these problems and to evolve his own answers to the question of human responsibility. The factor that remains constant, at every level of the playwright's presentation, is *search,* the quest for meaning. The essential question is posed by Gutman (Block II, p. 16): "'What is this place? Where are we? What is the meaning of—*Shhhh!*'—Ha, ha. . . ."

There are three levels of explication in *Camino Real.* Williams effects the synthesis of a basically American form of lyric drama with two other modes of expression: with the neo-Horatian dialogic form and with the morality play, most recently employed by the expressionists. In Williams' form, these three modes of development account for three levels of explication: (1) for the lyric stream of images, (2) for the synthetic myth, and (3) for the superimposition of a didactic, even theological, purpose. The playwright does not seem to have succeeded in fully integrating his sensible, rational, and transcendental levels of interpretation. Nevertheless, the play represents a significant achievement in the development of a mature contemporary form. Many of its essential characteristics have reappeared since 1953 in the drama of other playwrights in world theatre, especially in the work of Samuel Beckett, Eugène Ionesco, Jean Genêt, Harold Pinter, and Edward Albee, *Camino Real* will undoubtedly remain a significant example of Williams' developing form.

13. *Ibid.,* p. 8.

chapter seven

WILLIAMS AND THE MORAL FUNCTION

In the middle of the journey of our life I came to myself in a dark wood where the straight way was lost.

One of the most controversial aspects of the theatre of Tennessee Williams is the playwright's interpretation of moral responsibility in the drama. Although by his own admission Williams is deeply concerned with the ethical function of theatre, he continues, nevertheless, to attack many of the conventional codes on which life in Western societies is predicated.[1] Like Ibsen, Strindberg, Chekhov, Tolstoy, and George Bernard Shaw, Williams has used the theatre as a platform—if not, indeed, as a pulpit.[2] The Bochum critics describe *Camino Real*—

NOTE: This passage from Canto I of the *Inferno* is the epigraph which prefaces the published version of *Camino Real.*

1. See the Preface to *Sweet Bird of Youth,* pp. vii–xi.

2. The Bochum critics claim that in *Camino Real* Williams has obscured much of his moral and ethical content behind sensuous and—in the case of

like Strindberg's *To Damascus,* Ibsen's *Brand,* Kafka's *The Trial,* and Claudel's *The Satin Slipper*—as a sermon. It may be said that *A Streetcar Named Desire, Summer and Smoke, Cat on a Hot Tin Roof, Orpheus Descending, Suddenly Last Summer, Sweet Bird of Youth,* and *The Night of the Iguana* are, no less, morality plays.

Some of the controversy surrounding this aspect of the playwright's work may be traced to his anti-classic vision of the moral universe. Like other contemporary dramatists—particularly like the expressionist and post-expressionist writers—Williams interprets the human dilemma in the twentieth century as a "crisis of conscience," as a growing conflict within human consciousness, individual and collective. For the playwright, this crisis does not stem primarily from those failings controlled by conventional social, political, intellectual, and religious codes. Williams—like the great "Christian" poets, Dante, Shakespeare, and Racine—is primarily concerned with the exposure of the supraintellectual and suprasocietal deadly sins: pride, covetousness, lust, anger, gluttony, envy, and sloth. Like these dramatists, he is committed to an ethic which regards man as a sinner, as a transgressor whose salvation is dependent on his personal recognition of his condition. For Williams, as for Dante, the theatre is by nature committed to an extremely important task. Its essential purpose is to show man the root of his suffering: its function, to play out humanity's crisis, to give its tortured consciousness concrete shape.

Camino Real—obscure symbols. It seems correct to say that Williams, unlike Miller, usually states his ideas obliquely; that is, he incorporates them into the sensuous fabric of the work itself. However, in some cases he gives direct explication to content. In these instances he is inclined to employ the dramatic monologue, a device favored by O'Neill, Wilder, and Miller, as well as by the stream-of-consciousness novelists. Such monologues are given by Chance Wayne in *Sweet Bird of Youth,* Act I, pp. 38–39, 40, 41. Similar "sermons" on moral issues are given by Tom in *The Glass Menagerie,* Scene V, pp. 46–47; by Blanche in *A Streetcar Named Desire,* Scene II, p. 45; Scene IV, pp. 80–81; Scene X, p. 145; by Alma in *Summer and Smoke,* Scene I, pp. 18 and 30; Scene VI, p. 73; by Vee in *Orpheus Descending,* Scene II, pp. 90–92; by Catharine in *Suddenly Last Summer,* Scene II, p. 40; and by Shannon in *The Night of the Iguana,* Act II, pp. 55–57.

This motive has influenced Williams, like other contemporary dramatists, to reject much of the conventional system upon which the Greek drama of Sophocles was based. Williams and others, convinced of the limitations of classical ethical systems in a democratic society, have attempted to recover and to discover other perceptions capable of affecting human behavior at its unreasoning roots. There has, therefore, grown up in the late nineteenth and twentieth centuries a theatre of the irrational: the drama of Ibsen, Strindberg, and Shaw; of André Gide, Guillaume Apollinaire, Alfred Jarry, Jean Cocteau and Albert Camus; and, more recently, of Samuel Beckett, Eugène Ionesco, Jean Genêt, Harold Pinter, and Edward Albee. It is to this theatre that Williams belongs.[3] For like these writers, he proposes to shock the spectator into recognition of his moral condition by exposing both his public and private sins.

Williams, like André Gide, reveals his own morality by declaring his protagonist "immoral." But if Williams is indeed a moral writer, he clothes his ethic in parti-colored garments. We have noted his construction of a synthetic myth which employs aspects of Christian iconology in the explication of contemporary problems. But there are, in his symbolic structure, many other forms. One of the most disturbing of these, to American critics especially, has been his use of a vivid and comprehensive sexual symbology. It is commonly asserted that sexual delinquency, a subject which has had extended treatment in the work of Williams, had not, prior to 1945, been considered appropriate thematic material for the popular art of theatre. A review of the history of the theatre is enlightening in this regard; contrary to the assertion, sexual delinquency has always been an element of theme in Western drama. It is, indeed, the main theme of *Oedipus Rex* and is a persistent element of content in the theatre of Shakespeare. In the American

3. Eric Bentley calls this theatre "magical." Antonin Artaud has described it as "the theatre of cruelty." I should like to designate it as "the theatre of shock." For its intent is to produce catharsis through a primitive technique which modern psychotherapy still employs: through giving concrete shape to the "demons" which haunt man.

theatre, O'Neill's study of the prostitute Anna Christie predated Williams' portrait of Blanche DuBois by some twenty-five years. The problem with Williams, as with Ibsen and Strindberg, appears to rest in a more fundamental and highly affecting aesthetic problem. For the playwright seems to suggest that the spectacle to which he gives shape is the normative image of man; that is, Williams posits his delinquent anti-hero as the true image of the moral and spiritual life of modern man.

Actually, the moral philosophy reflected in the drama of Tennessee Williams is not singular; his image of man is the approximation of a contour appearing in the work of a wide range of contemporaries, including such "Christian dramatists" as Paul Claudel, T. S. Eliot, Christopher Fry, and others, as well as such secular playwrights as Bertolt Brecht, Jean Giraudoux, Jean Cocteau, Jean Anouilh, and Jean-Paul Sartre. Indeed, Sartre has written that it is, today, the theatre which has usurped the function of the church in giving moral sanction to the life of man:

> . . . The theatre will be able to present man in his entirety only in proportion to the theatre's willingness to be *moral*. By that we do not mean that it should put forward examples illustrating the rules of deportment or the practical ethics taught to children, but rather that the study of the conflict of characters should be replaced by the presentation of the conflict of rights. . . . In each case it is, in the final analysis and in spite of divergent interests, the system of values, of ethics and of concepts of man which are lined up against each other.[4]

Christian dramatists such as Eliot claim that contemporary theatre has simply recovered its theological function: the naming, exploration, interpretation, and ordering of experience. From this point of view, it may be interpreted that Williams uses a sexual symbology as an element of language, as a kind of glass through which he focuses on his dark vision of man.

Williams' early universe, like that of William Faulkner's, is fundamentally that of primeval man. In plays such as *Battle of Angels* (1941) the dramatist has attempted to delve beneath

4. Sartre, "Forgers of Myth" (*Theatre Arts,* XXX [June, 1946]), pp. 329–30.

the successive masks of civilizations and to examine man's primitive state of consciousness: to re-create that which Jung has described as the "original structural conditions of the psyche." In *Battle of Angels,* an early version of *Orpheus Descending,* he creates such a universe—a world as old as man himself. In this symbolic world of the rural South, Williams is concerned about something not unlike original sin. He traces a pattern of transgression which engulfs an entire community. He follows the tragic progress of a young musician who unwittingly sets off a chain reaction of human cruelties. However, as the playwright develops, a more sophisticated moral exposition gradually begins to emerge. In *The Glass Menagerie,* his primordial universe is superseded by a world of more ambiguous proportions. Indeed, as we shall see, his primal universe collides with a second world called "civilization."

A study of the whole fabric of Williams' work seems to show a conscious pattern of moral development. If he is concerned in the early plays with the justification of the poetic function, he is in the later dramas committed primarily to defining a more comprehensive moral responsibility. The first plays may be said to reflect the moral attitude of the romantics; that is, in works such as *The Glass Menagerie* Williams seems to be primarily committed to the Nietzschean "ethic of self-realization."[5] There is, especially in *The Glass Menagerie,* the romantic suggestion that art is itself the transcendent mode of salvation. Throughout the early plays, there seems little doubt that Williams regards art as a kind of "transmorality," the only salvation for an insensitive and unseeing humanity.

In plays such as *The Lady of Larkspur Lotion,* it is the artist who discerns the truth of human suffering, who correctly per-

5. This interest differentiates the motive of Williams from that of Miller. If Williams—like Eugene O'Neill—has been concerned with the individually-oriented universe, Miller, the rationalist, has fixed his interest in society. His conscious motivation is in part defined in an essay "On Social Plays," Preface to *A View from the Bridge* (London, 1960), pp. 7–24.

ceives civilization's moral crisis. A character describing himself as "Anton Pavlov Chekhov" delivers this sermon to the unsympathetic landlady Mrs. Wire as he attempts to dissuade her from persecuting the luckless "Lady of Larkspur Lotion":

> [S]uppose that I, to make this nightmare bearable for as long as I must continue to be the helpless protagonist of it—suppose that I ornament, illuminate—glorify it! With dreams and fictions and fancies! Such as the existence of a 780-page masterpiece—impending Broadway productions—marvelous volumes of verse in the hands of publishers only waiting for signatures to release them! Suppose that I live in this world of pitiful fiction! What satisfaction can it give you, good woman, to tear it to pieces, to crush it—call it a *lie*? I tell you this—now listen! There are no lies but the lies that are stuffed in the mouth by the hard-knuckled hand of need, the cold iron fist of necessity, Mrs. Wire! So I am a liar, yes! But your world is built on a lie, your world is a hideous fabrication of lies! Lies! Lies! . . . Now I'm tired and I've said my say and I have no money to give you so get away and leave this woman in peace! Leave her alone. Go on, get out, get away!
>
> (In 27 *Wagons Full of Cotton,* pp. 70–71)

Williams' early plays are one-movement studies of people caught in the ambiguous world of the twentieth century. Williams, as poet, looks at a group of these mutilated people. But he looks at their inner lives. He attempts to intuit their feelings and to record the results of his poetic exploration. His compassionate study has resulted in many poignant accounts. An early record of Blanche DuBois—*Portrait of a Madonna*[6]—is among the plays of this group. Similarly, a preliminary study of the girl "Laura" in *The Glass Menagerie* appears in a short story, *Portrait of a Girl in Glass.*[7] In the short work *27 Wagons Full of Cotton,*[8] a play later made into the film *Baby Doll,* Williams shows the corrosive effect of the materialistic "ethic" in the rural South. In his early exploration of this theme, a subject which finds extended development in *Cat on a Hot Tin Roof* and *Sweet Bird of Youth,* he records the progressive dehumani-

6. In 27 *Wagons Full of Cotton,* pp. 89–104.
7. In *One Arm and Other Stories,* pp. 97–112.
8. In 27 *Wagons Full of Cotton,* pp. 3–28.

zation of a cotton merchant in the mythical town of Blue Mountain, Mississippi. Jake Meighan, his wife Flora, and the Superintendent Silva Vicarro are figures reflecting a moral distortion comparable to that apparent in the visual studies of expressionists such as Erich Heckel or Emil Nolde.

A singularly poignant image is the ancient and courtly salesman Mr. Charlie Cotton, who appears in *The Last of My Solid Gold Watches.* Mr. Charlie, a precursor of Willy Loman, is the image of man discarded as an "obsolete model" by a rapidly advancing technology. Mr. Charlie describes the condition which has led to his destruction in time:

> Mortality, that was the trouble! Some people think that millions now living are never going to *die.* I don't think that—I think it's a misapprehension not borne out by the facts! We go like flies when we come to the end of the summer . . . And who is going to prevent it? (*He becomes depressed.*) Who—is going—to prevent it! (*He nods gravely.*) The road is changed. The shoe industry is changed. These times are—revolution! (*He rises and moves to the window.*) I don't like the way that it looks. You can take it from me—the world that I used to know—the world that this boy's father used t'know—the world we belonged to, us old time war-horses!—is slipping and sliding away from under our shoes. Who is going to prevent it?
>
> (In 27 *Wagons Full of Cotton,* p. 81)

Mr. Charlie defines "existential dread" in the language of his rural upbringing:

> Meaning—unknown—to men of my generation! The rudeness—the lack of respect—the newspapers full of strange items! The terrible—fast—dark—rush of events in the world! Toward what and where and why! . . . I don't pretend to have any knowledge of now! I only say—and I say this very humbly—I don't understand—what's happened. . . . I'm one of them monsters you see reproduced in museums—out of the dark old ages—the giant *rep*-tiles, and the dino-whatever-you-call-ems. BUT—I *do* know *this!* And I state it without any shame! Initiative—self-reliance—independence of character! The old sterling qualities that distinguished one man from another—the clay from the potters—the potters from the clay—are—(*kneading the air with his hands*) How is it the old song goes? . . . Gone with the roses of *yesterday.* Yes—with the *wind!* (Pages 83–84)

His younger companion comments on the futility of existence:

In the papers they print people *dead* in one corner and people *born* in the next and usually *one* just about levels *off* with the *other*.
(Page 84)

Mr. Charlie responds with a valuation of technological progress:

My point is this: the ALL-LEATHER slogan is not what sells any more —not in shoes and not in humanity, neither! The emphasis isn't on quality. Production, production, yes! But out of inferior goods! *Ersatz!* —that's what they're making 'em out of! (Page 84)

His summation of the present condition of man is given in the closing lines of the play:

[I]t ain't even late in the day any more—(*He throws up the blind.*) It's NIGHT! (*The space of the window is black.*) (Page 85)

Throughout the plays of these early series, vignettes such as *Hello from Bertha, Talk to Me Like The Rain and Let Me Listen,* and *Moony's Kid Don't Cry,* Williams studies the fate of the unfortunate in the ambiguous moral universe of the twentieth century. Like the Jacobeans, he sees man besieged by history, destroyed by the very progress which has brought him the advantages of modern life. For Williams, the movement of time and history is corrosive. Progress in the twentieth century has brought with it—as it has in other epochs of human existence—great personal suffering, a comprehensive moral and spiritual decay.

Williams turns his attention in his longer works to the causes of suffering in the modern world. *The Glass Menagerie, Summer and Smoke, The Rose Tattoo,* and *Cat on a Hot Tin Roof* are concerned with the effect of social, political, and cultural transition upon the individual. In *The Glass Menagerie,* the focus of this conflict is individual and personal. The poet-figure Tom is engaged in making a decision about his ethos, his "style of life." In this play, the ethical frame is extremely narrow; Tom's view of moral responsibility is, in the main, shaped by the romantic imperative of "self-expression." In the plays which follow, however, there is a rapid extension of the frame of reference which surrounds the individual's choice of a life-order. In *A Streetcar Named Desire* the playwright traces several styles of life, each to its poetic termination: that of Blanche, that of Stanley, and that of the "indifferent" Stella. Unlike *The Glass Menagerie,* the frame of reference in *A Streetcar Named Desire* is primarily social; for individual choices affect the entire world in which the protagonist lives. Thus it is that Blanche's life-order has been, in some measure, dictated by the circumstances which she has inherited. More important is the fact that her moral choices continue to affect the lives of others. Indeed, there is in this drama a severe and brutal struggle between Blanche and Stanley. They engage each other in mortal combat for the lives of Stella, Mitch, and even for that of the child yet unborn. Perhaps the crux of the moral dilemma in this play is that neither of these antagonists represents an even remotely acceptable moral choice. As a moral essay, then, *A Streetcar Named Desire* is incomplete. The author states the problem, explores its ramifications, but cannot—or at least does not—arrive at a true resolution of the issues which he has raised. Apparently at some point Williams became aware of the moral inconclusiveness of this drama, for in the succeeding play he returned to the exploration of what is essentially the same issue.

Summer and Smoke both enlarges the scope of the moral dilemma and gives it more systematic explication. In this work, Williams poses an image of a human being—with possibilities for moral commitment—at an earlier age. The "camera" catches Alma at the very moment of transition between morality and decadence, in a reversal of the process of becoming. We watch her transformed, on the stage, from a Corneillian heroine, devoted to love, duty, honor, and chastity, to a Racinian woman, torn by insatiable desires and inner longings. Williams illustrates, in her personal disintegration, the crisis of modern civilization: its inability to choose, finally, between the lofty ideals of the humanistic tradition and the materialistic values given systematic explication by the great nineteenth-century determinists. Williams symbolizes this radical choice in his metaphor "Summer and Smoke." He personifies these alternatives in Alma and her opposite, Dr. John Buchanan. Williams describes the doctor in this language:

> [. . . *He is now a Promethean figure, brilliantly and restlessly alive in a stagnant society. The excess of his power has not yet found a channel. If it remains without one, it will burn him up. At present he is unmarked by the dissipations in which he relieves his demoniac unrest; he has the fresh and shining look of an epic hero. . . .*]
> (Scene I, pp. 8–9)

The "Promethean" doctor, then, is another of Williams' throwbacks to the primal condition of man: to "epic" consciousness. Buchanan's ethical sense, like that of the Homeric heroes, relates primarily to self-creation—to survival, sensual gratification, and a limited sense of self-expression. He describes life in these "Olympian" terms:

> Now listen here to the anatomy lecture! This upper story's the brain which is hungry for something called truth and doesn't get much but keeps on feeling hungry! This middle's the belly which is hungry for food. This part down here is the sex which is hungry for love because it is sometimes lonesome. I've fed all three, as much of all three as I could or as much as I wanted—You've fed none—nothing. Well—maybe your belly a little—watery subsistance—But love or truth, nothing but —nothing but hand-me-down notions!—attitudes!—poses! Now you can go. The anatomy lecture is over. (Scene VIII, p. 95)

Buchanan, despite his upper-middle class status, is another Stanley, a man who believes in the fundamental morality of a primitive existence—in the "ethic" of primal man. Like Stanley, he expresses contempt for the abstractions of the historical, cultural, and traditional past. But Buchanan cannot be described as a fulfilled human being. Despite his declaration that he has fed himself, he seems not to have found any greater degree of self-realization than has Alma. He is, on the contrary, driven by his demons of desire to destruction. He is a failure as a doctor, as a son, and as a human being, until he is redeemed by the love of the young girl Nell (Scene XI, p. 118).

Williams suggests, however, that the moral failures of John Buchanan are yet more acceptable to society than the spiritual eccentricities of Alma Winemiller. For Alma, from her childhood, has been given to the contemplation of the life of the soul, a function which has no reality in the world in which she lives. Williams describes her (Scene I, p. 15) as an "eighteenth-century heroine." She yearns to play out the role of the genteel heroine of sentimental drama. Ironically, Alma gives expression to all of the ideals to which modern society still claims allegiance: to fidelity, filial piety, selflessness, discipline, love of truth, respect for tradition, and an inspired sense of dedication to human service. She describes the humanist symbol—the Gothic cathedral—in a way that reflects her identification with its longing, its aspiration:

> How everything reaches up, how everything seems to be straining for something out of the reach of stone—or human—fingers? . . . The immense stained windows, the great arched doors that are five or six times the height of the tallest man—the vaulted ceiling and all the delicate spires—all reaching up to something beyond attainment! To me—well, that is the secret, the principle back of existence—the everlasting struggle and aspiration for more than our human limits have placed in our reach. . . Who was that said that—oh, so beautiful thing!—"All of us are in the gutter, but some of us are looking at the stars!"
>
> (Scene VI, p. 73)

The humanitarian Alma tries to persuade John of his vocation in medicine:

> Most of us have no choice but to lead useless lives! But you have a gift for scientific research! You have a chance to serve humanity. Not just to go on enduring for the sake of endurance, but to serve a noble, humanitarian cause, to relieve human suffering. And what do you do about it? Everything that you can to alienate the confidence of nice people who love and respect your father. While he is devoting himself to the fever at Lyon you drive your automobile at a reckless pace from

one disorderly roadhouse to another! You say you have seen two things through the microscope, anarchy and order? Well, obviously, *order* is not the thing that impressed you . . . conducting yourself like some overgrown schoolboy who wants to be known as the wildest fellow in town! And you—a gifted young doctor—*Magna cum Laude!* You know what I call it? I call it a *desecration!* (Scene I, p. 30)

The moral contradiction within modern life is revealed in the fact that Alma is destroyed, despite the supposed nobility of her ideals, and the irresponsible Buchanan is, indeed, rewarded. The collapse of moral order in Alma's world is even more clearly reflected in her admiration of characteristics which are, by her own definition, weaknesses:

I've lived next door to you all the days of my life, a weak and divided person who stood in adoring awe of your singleness, of your strength. And that is my story! (Scene XI, p. 119)

Alma is correct in her perception that the tragic element in the world of her existence is its division: it is a fragmentation that has affected everyone in the play. Her description may well be applied to each character in his turn:

Oh, I suppose I am sick, one of those weak and divided people who slip like shadows among you solid strong ones. But sometimes, out of necessity, we shadowy people take on a strength of our own.
(Scene XI, pp. 118–19)

In *The Rose Tattoo,* Williams retreats from these hard realities to the relative safety of a quasi-romantic world. Around the heroine Serafina he composes an essay on the "noble savage" of romantic description. But the completion of life which Serafina experiences may be attributed to the play's detachment from actuality. Set in a mythical Sicilian village off the Gulf Coast of Mobile, the drama is taken out of the modern world and is set, in effect, in another century. The remote fishing village is reminiscent of those of nineteenth-century Italy, Spain, France, or Ireland. Like certain of the plays of Synge, O'Casey, and Lady Gregory, *The Rose Tattoo* is a romantic essay on a life which has passed, a life whose tranquility may have existed only in the poetic imagination of those who saw it as observers.

With his return to the harsh world of the twentieth century, Williams again takes up the question of moral conflict. *Cat on a Hot Tin Roof* is an intricate development of the subject of moral choice. In this play Williams not only explores the problem of choice, he raises related questions which are ontological and epistemological in nature.[9] Williams suggests, in *Cat on a Hot Tin Roof* (Act I, pp. 37–38), that a serious conflict of "truths" rages within reality itself. He defines the subject of this play as "mendacity": the condition of falsity. The problem of "appearance versus reality," a theme in early works such as *The Glass Menagerie,* thus becomes seriously complicated. For in the later play, Williams has determined that affective reality—the reality of everyday life—is in the nature of things misleading, illusory, and, ultimately, false.

Eugene O'Neill has explored the subject of appearance and reality in his long study of human illusion and disillusion: *The Iceman Cometh.*[10] But O'Neill, in his work, suggests that there is, somewhere in the world of human experience, a concrete truth which may be grasped by those who have stamina enough to confront it. In *Cat on a Hot Tin Roof* Williams seems to say, on the contrary, that there is no truth at all in existence, that the very nature of experience conspires against human understanding. He develops this theme in three movements. The first of these progressions mirrors the anguish of the protagonist Brick, seeking to unravel the truth of his complicity in the death of his friend Skipper. The second variation is in thematic proximity; for it concerns the life relationship between Brick and his wife Maggie. The third is, like the first, an extremely ambiguous progression. It involves the attempt

9. It is possible to describe certain interests of *Camino Real* as eschatological in nature; for Williams posits in "Kilroy" a savior of humanity, a man who sets the "water of life to flowing again in the mountains." See *Camino Real,* pp. 5 and 159–61.

10. Eugene O'Neill, *The Iceman Cometh* (New York, 1946).

to diagnose Big Daddy's cancer. The ambiguity of this illness symbolizes the whole problem of the play; for it poses the crucial question, not only about Big Daddy Pollitt, but also about the whole of mankind. What is the nature of its illness? Is it a sickness unto death?

In *Cat on a Hot Tin Roof* Williams suggests that the sickness in the House of Pollitt, like that of humanity, may be traced to its belief in illusions. Big Daddy has believed in the power of money. He speaks of its failure as a god:

> It's lucky I'm a rich man, it sure is lucky, well, I'm a rich man, Brick, yep, I'm a mighty rich man.
>
> [*His eyes light up for a moment.*]
>
> Y'know how much I'm worth? Guess, Brick! Guess how much I'm worth!
>
> [*Brick smiles vaguely over his drink.*]
>
> Close on ten million in cash an' blue chip stocks, outside, mind you, of twenty-eight thousand acres of the richest land this side of the valley Nile!
>
> [*A puff and crackle and the night sky blooms with an eerie greenish glow. Children shriek on the gallery.*]
>
> But a man can't buy his life with it, he can't buy back his life with it when his life has been spent, that's one thing not offered in the Europe fire-sale or in the American markets or any markets on earth, a man can't buy his life with it, he can't buy back his life when his life is finished. . . .
>
> That's a sobering thought, a very sobering thought, and that's a thought that I was turning over in my head, over and over and over—until today. . . .
>
> I'm wiser and sadder, Brick, for this experience which I just gone through. (Act II, pp. 70–71)

Although Big Daddy is disillusioned about the power of money, Maggie the "Cat" still believes in this god:

> MARGARET: Always had to suck up to people I couldn't stand because they had money and I was poor as Job's turkey. You don't know what that's like. Well, I'll tell you, it's like you would feel a thousand miles away from Echo Spring!—And had to get back to it on that broken ankle . . . without a crutch!
>
> That's how it feels to be as poor as Job's turkey and have to suck up to relatives that you hated because they had money and all you had was a

bunch of hand-me-down clothes and a few old moldy three per cent government bonds. My daddy loved his liquor, he fell in love with his liquor the way you've fallen in love with Echo Spring!—And my poor Mama, having to maintain some semblance of social position, to keep appearances up, on an income of one hundred and fifty dollars a month on those old government bonds!

When I came out, the year that I made my debut, I had just two evening dresses! One Mother made me from a pattern in *Vogue,* the other a hand-me-down from a snotty rich cousin I hated!

—The dress that I married you in was my grandmother's weddin' gown. . . .

So that's why I'm like a cat on a hot tin roof! (Act I, pp. 37–38)

But Brick has been the victim of an equally devastating illusion. He has worshipped the false "god of youth":

Maggie declares that Skipper and I went into pro-football after we left "Ole Miss" because we were scared to grow up. . .

[*He moves downstage with the shuffle and clop of a cripple on a crutch. As Margaret did when her speech became "recitative," he looks out into the house, commanding its attention by his direct concentrated gaze—a broken "tragically elegant" figure telling simply as much as he knows of "the Truth":*]

—Wanted to—keep on tossing—those long, long!—high, high!—passes that—couldn't be intercepted except by time, the aerial attack that made us famous! And so we did, we did, we kept it up for one season, that aerial attack, we held it high!—Yeah, but—

—that summer, Maggie, she laid the law down to me, said, Now or never, and so I married Maggie. . . (Act II, p. 106)

In the end, only the life-force propels the House of Pollitt onward. Williams concludes the Broadway production with these lines from Maggie the Cat:

Oh, you weak, beautiful people who give up with such grace. What you need is someone to take hold of you—gently, with love, and hand your life back to you, like something gold you let go of—and I can! I'm determined to do it—and nothing's more determined than a cat on a tin roof—is there? Is there, baby?

(Act III, p. 197—Broadway version)

In *Cat on a Hot Tin Roof,* Williams details a kind of existence which is by this time familiar. In *Camino Real,* however, he makes a definitive change in his articulation of the moral universe. In this play—actually an earlier work than *Cat on a Hot Tin Roof*—he extends the ground of being. *Camino Real* represents an attempt to rise out of the plane of the mundane. Williams begins, slowly, to transcend human despair, suffering, division, loneliness, dread, and failure through an appeal to the Christlike virtues of pity, tenderness, sympathy, forebearance, and forgiveness. He seems, finally, to conclude that there is within the universe a power which can transcend the ambiguous nature of man. *Camino Real* suggests that humanity may be saved through commitment—on the part of the individual and society alike—to a simple but rigorous ethic: to sympathy for others and to confrontation of oneself.

In the group of plays written since 1955, Williams seems to have been engaged in exploring the implications contingent on the application of his transmoral doctrine. In a discussion of the moral function in his theatre, the playwright wrote in the Foreword to *Sweet Bird of Youth:*

> When I came to my writing desk on a recent morning, I found lying on my desk top an unmailed letter that I had written. I began reading it and found this sentence: "We are all civilized people, which means that we are all savages at heart but observing a few amenities of civilized behavior." Then I went on to say: "I am afraid that I observe fewer of these amenities than you do. Reason? My back is to the wall and has been to the wall for so long that the pressure of my back on the wall has started to crumble the plaster that covers the bricks and mortar."
> (Foreword, p. vii)

Williams suggests that this condition is, indeed, universal.

> Since I am a member of the human race, when I attack its behavior toward fellow members I am obviously including myself in the attack, unless I regard myself as not human but superior to humanity. I don't. In fact, I can't expose a human weakness on the stage unless I know it through having it myself. I have exposed a good many human weaknesses and brutalities and consequently I have them. (Foreword, p. x)

The playwright examines the question of human transgression as it is treated in his work:

Guilt is universal. I mean a strong sense of guilt. If there exists any area in which a man can rise above his moral condition, imposed upon him at birth and long before birth, by the nature of his breed, then I think it is only a willingness to know it, to face its existence in him, and I think that at least below the conscious level, we all face it.

(Foreword, p. x)

Williams' later plays appear to be concerned with his attempt to codify his transmorality: with an effort to formulate a stringent ethic which is relevant to the everyday world of human affairs. In *Orpheus Descending,* the final version of *Battle of Angels,* the terms of this contemporary ethic begin to come into focus. In both works, the incident which is the subject of the action is the lynching of the young musician, Val Xavier. In the earlier work, Williams gives an account of the events leading to the murder and intersperses direct comments on the moral questions involved. In the later version he submerges much of this discursive content in his mythic structure. He equates the appearance of the young guitarist to the journey of Orpheus to the underworld and to the descent of Christ into hell. Williams explores the correspondences between the psychic life of the town, the frenzy of the Bacchantes, and the fever for crucifixion which gripped the Jerusalem of Jesus' day. The story of the musician thus takes on the aspect of an archaic mystery. The "dark god" brings music, enchantment, and fertility to the dying town. For these gifts he is sacrificed in the necessary primitive ritual.

With his myth of the "dying god," a symbol on which he turns any number of contents, Williams seeks to expose the ruthless savagery still extant in modern man. The play reveals the interrelationship of exploitation, suspicion, hate, and cruelty in the precipitation of group violence. The playwright explores the complicity of each character in the murder of the protagonist. He studies the roots of this moral disaster in social ills. He shows the death of Val to be the climax of an entire complex of transgressions which, in the private and public consciousnesses of the community, required a victim.

Williams, like Faulkner, provides important psychological insight into the anatomy of violence. He gives concrete shape to the mind and spirit of the psychic underworld. In Act Three of *Orpheus Descending,* the Sheriff speaks to Val:

> But I'm gonna tell you something. They's a certain county I know of which has a big sign at the county line that says "Nigger, don't let the sun go down on you in this county." That's all it says, it don't threaten nothing, it just says, "Nigger, don't let the sun go down on you in this county!"
>
> [*Chuckles hoarsely. Rises and takes a step toward Val.*]
>
> Well, son! You ain't a nigger and this is not that county, but, son, I want you to just imagine that you seen a sign that said to you: "Boy, don't let the sun rise on you in this county." . . . 'S that understood now, boy? . . . I *hope* so. I don't like *violence.*
>
> (Act III, Scene 2, pp. 96–97)

In *Orpheus Descending,* as in other works, Williams uncovers the Dionysian consciousness which yet lives and thrives in modern America. He confirms the understanding of theology as well as that of modern thought in suggesting that these archaic drives have not been bred out of civilized man.

The taste for cruelty is not, however, limited to his mythic Mississippi town. In *Suddenly Last Summer* Williams explores the problem of inhumanity supported by social, political, and intellectual advantages. In *Suddenly Last Summer* he demonstrates that intelligence and morality are not necessarily properties of the same function. This work, in many ways the most terrifying of this playwright's apprehensions, shows man the prisoner of a corrupt intelligence. The gifted, intelligent, and attractive Mrs. Venable is, no less than the primitive creatures of the earlier drama, a savage. Indeed, she is a more frightening creature than the Sheriff, for she is committed to the annihilation of a fellow human being through the agencies of society. Moreover, she has built up an elaborate and impressive rationalization to obscure her anticipated crime:

> Name it that—I don't care—. There's just two things to remember. She's a destroyer. My son was a *creator!*—Now if my honesty's shocked you—pick up your little black bag without the subsidy in it, and run

away from this garden!—Nobody's heard our conversation but you and I, Doctor Sugar. . . . (Scene I, p. 32)

Williams poses in this drama an extremely serious question for civilization; it involves the threat that the humanity symbolized by Mrs. Venable may come to control society itself. The question of the morality of the prefrontal lobotomy serves the playwright as a stage for exploring the responsibility of the family, of the church, and of organized medicine in a civilized state. Strangely enough, in *Suddenly Last Summer* it is medicine which takes a moral view of social action. Catharine Holly's family—her fatuous mother and her weak brother—are examples of Williams' morally indifferent humanity; that is, they are unable to even consider the moral implications of another's destiny. The representative of the church, Sister Felicity, is momentarily sympathetic but essentially removed from the human struggle. It is the doctor who, in his concern for the girl, reveals a sense of commitment to moral principle.

It is in many ways, then, the doctor who stands at the center of the moral drama in *Suddenly Last Summer*. For it is he who is forced to weigh the truth of the girl's terrible story; it is he who must make the decision as to whether Catharine should be deprived of the "human ability" to suffer. It is he who is required to risk ambition, professional success, and perhaps even love in order to protect the human rights of a powerless individual. He gives the spectator some insight into his own conflict:

> My work is such a *new* and *radical* thing that people in charge of state funds are naturally a little scared of it and keep us on a small budget, so small that—. We need a separate ward for my patients, I need trained assistants, I'd like to marry a girl I can't afford to marry!—
> (Scene I, p. 29)

The doctor assumes a role which is, by reason of strength, different from that taken by Blanche DuBois. Despite all of the factors which urge him to become a tool of Mrs. Venable's vengeance, he maintains an essentially moral position. The lines of the play are a dramatic affirmation of the playwright's "new" belief in the possibility of goodness in some men:

[*Mrs. Venable springs with amazing power from her wheelchair, stumbles erratically but swiftly toward the girl and tries to strike her with her cane. The Doctor snatches it from her and catches her as she is about to fall. She gasps hoarsely several times as he leads her toward the exit.*]

MRS. VENABLE [*offstage*]: *Lion's View! State asylum, cut this hideous story out of her brain!*

[*Mrs. Holly sobs and crosses to George, who turns away from her, saying:*]

GEORGE: Mom, I'll quit school, I'll get a job, I'll—

MRS. HOLLY: Hush son! Doctor, can't you say something?

[*Pause. The Doctor comes downstage. Catherine wanders out into the garden followed by the Sister.*]

DOCTOR [*after a while, reflectively, into space*]: I think we ought at least to consider the possibility that the girl's story could be true. . . .

THE END (Scene IV, pp. 87–88)

In *Sweet Bird of Youth,* as in *Camino Real,* Williams gathers together a number of transgressors into a single world, where he ponders their destiny. The characters in this play are linked together by their common worship of the "god of success." In their pursuit of this illusion, these people have not only destroyed others, they have become phantoms—shadows of former selves. Like the characters in *Camino Real,* they have become lifeless images in a charade. The protagonist of *Sweet Bird of Youth,* Chance Wayne, describes life as a "parade." His highest ambition is to be a leading performer in this gilded procession. For the fading movie star, Alexandra del Lago, the performance is over; its pleasures can only be reinvoked by intoxicants. She describes the pain of having the illusion of success fade:

But I knew in my heart that the legend of Alexandra del Lago couldn't be separated from an appearance of youth. . . .

There's no more valuable knowledge than knowing the right time to go. I knew it. I went at the right time to go. *RETIRED!* Where to? To what? To that dead planet the moon. . . .

> There's nowhere else to retire to when you retire from an art because, believe it or not, I really was once an artist. So I retired to the moon, but the atmosphere of the moon doesn't have any oxygen in it. I began to feel breathless, in that withered, withering country, of time coming after time not meant to come after. . . . (Scene I, p. 23)

Alexandra del Lago describes her own inner condition:

> Well, sooner or later, at some point in your life, the thing that you lived for is lost or abandoned, and then . . . you die, or find something else. (Scene I, p. 25)

Alexandra del Lago's decadence is matched by that of the young man Chance Wayne, who regards himself as a commodity to be bought and sold on the open market to the highest bidder.

The belief in the illusion of success has been no less devastating to the inhabitants of Gulf City, Chance Wayne's former home. Here, Williams shows the extended influence of false values in public life as he exposes the vast operation of the political machine dominated by Boss Finley. In his portraits of the Finley clan, Boss, his son Tom Junior, and their supporters, the playwright creates Dantean studies of men guilty of the mortal "Sins of the Wolf." [11] These fraudulent ones are more despicable for their complicity in the destruction of a "good" human being. Heavenly Finley, the daughter of the political boss, is annihilated in the struggle between two equally corrupt sides. In *Sweet Bird of Youth* the moral destruction is almost total. There is in this drama, however, one hopeful sign. It is the confrontation of the anti-heroic Chance with destiny. Threatened with the ultimate violence—castration—Chance finally confronts his past and accepts responsibility for his transgressions against humanity. The playwright writes of him:

11. The Bochum critics suggest this parallelism. Williams' theology seems definitely to follow Christian lines of development. His view of man is similar to that of St. Augustine. But more interesting, perhaps, is his construction of a catalogue of sins which is similar to that of Dante. Like Dante, Williams attributes to the great sinners the error of fraudulence. Moreover, like New Testament writers, he regards the sins of the flesh—the venial sins—as less mortal than the sins of the spirit: pride, covetousness, anger, fraudulence, and mendacity.

[*Note: in this area it is very important that* CHANCE's *attitude should be self-recognition but* not *self-pity—a sort of deathbed dignity and honesty apparent in it. In both* CHANCE *and the* PRINCESS, *we should return to the huddling-together of the lost, but not with sentiment, which is false, but with whatever is truthful in the moments when people share doom, face firing squads together. Because the* PRINCESS *is really equally doomed. She can't turn back the clock any more than can* CHANCE, *and the clock is equally relentless to them both. . . . Both are faced with castration, and in her heart she knows it. They sit side by side on the bed like two passengers on a train sharing a bench.*]

(Act III, p. 112)

Chance finds peace in penitence:

I didn't know there was a clock in this room.

. . . .

It goes tick-tick, it's quieter than your heart-beat, but it's slow dynamite, a gradual explosion, blasting the world we lived in to burnt-out pieces. . . . Time—who could beat it, who could defeat it ever? Maybe some saints and heroes, but not Chance Wayne. I lived on something, that—time?

. . . .

. . . Gnaws away, like a rat gnaws off its own foot caught in a trap, and then, with its foot gnawed off and the rat set free, couldn't run, couldn't go, bled and died. . . . (Act III, p. 113)

The protagonist, in his curtain speech, identifies his destiny with that of all men:

CHANCE [*rising and advancing to the forestage*]:—I don't ask for your pity, but just for your understanding—not even that—no. Just for your recognition of me in you, and the enemy, time, in us all.

[*The curtain closes.*]

THE END (Act III, p. 114)

Williams, in these later plays, exposes the effect of private immorality upon society. He traces the corrosive influence of immoral action on individual destiny, family life, commerce, and politics, and shows its threat to society and to social institutions as well as to individual well-being. In his last works, he begins to show some progress toward a limited solution of human ills. In the short play *Period of Adjustment,* he considers in more compassionate terms than before the relationship between men and women. He poses in this play a compromise between hate and the violent passions which have in his works wracked relationships between the sexes. The couple in this "serious comedy" find that the healing grace, the bond between them, is something akin to sympathy. Williams describes this gentle emotion as "tenderness." His epigraph to the play speaks of this reconciliation:

> For tenderness I would lay down
> The weapon that holds death away,
> But little words of tenderness
> Are those I never learned to say. (Page 1)

It is the growth of tenderness for mankind which is the theme of *The Night of the Iguana.* If the earlier works are studies of transgression, *The Night of the Iguana* is an essay on redemption. The anti-heroic Shannon finds reconciliation at the end of a long journey; he finds it, in part, through the intercession of two saintly souls: an aged poet and his compassionate granddaughter. Williams' later plays are distinguished from earlier works by the acceleration of his anti-hero's search for a mode of transcendence. Since *Camino Real,* it appears to have been God with whom his anti-hero has sought ultimate reconciliation. The "long dark night of the soul" seems to have brought the protagonist to a realization reminiscent of those of early Church fathers. Indeed, the "odyssey" of Williams' tortured anti-heroes often has the ring of the *Confessions of St. Augustine.*[12]

That it has been God whom the anti-hero has sought becomes clear in *Suddenly Last Summer.* Mrs. Venable, explaining the poetic journey, gives words to this claim:

12. Note, particularly, the account of Augustine's inner conflict in Book VIII of *The Confessions.* Augustine seeks to effect the same transcendence which the contemporary playwright desires: (1) to understand the nature of his inner conflict; (2) to objectify pain through confession; and (3) to transcend sin through a power greater than himself. If this power, in the early plays of Williams, is art, it is God for the aging protagonists of his later works.

All right, I started to say that my son was looking for God and I stopped myself because I was afraid that if I said he was looking for God, you'd say to yourself, "Oh, a pretentious young crack-pot!"—which Sebastian was not. All poets look for God, all good poets do, and they have to look harder for Him than priests do since they don't have the help of such famous guide-books and well-organized expeditions as priests have with their scriptures and churches. All right! Well, now I've said it, my son was looking for God. I mean for a clear image of Him. He spent that whole blazing equatorial day in the crow's nest of the schooner watching that thing on the beach of the Endantadas till it was too dark to see it, and when he came back down the rigging, he said, Well, now I've seen Him!—and he meant God. . . (Scene I, p. 21)

The vision of God has, as in scriptural literature, rendered the communicant Sebastian blind and delirious and left him with a conscious need for expiation.

The defrocked priest Shannon, in *The Night of the Iguana,* like the poet Sebastian, is a man in search of divine forgiveness. A rebel, thrown out of the established church for his heretical utterings, he is apparently conducting his own search—without benefit of "clerical guide-books." Shannon, like others of Williams' protagonists, is haunted by a sense of guilt—a guilt which he describes as a "spook." At times his burden becomes so oppressive that he grows violent and must be hospitalized. He makes in this play a full and extended confession of the transgressions which have alienated him from inner peace. But Shannon's sins are not, in Williams' view, deadly. He stands accused of venial faults. In Dante's symbology, he is guilty of the "Sins of the Leopard": lust and incontinence.[13] Shannon's sins, though more serious than that of Alma (futility), are less mortal than that of Big Daddy (fraudulence), and less binding yet than that of Boss Finley (treachery). He is not, therefore, forbidden the forgiveness for which he seeks.

In *The Night of the Iguana* Shannon describes his search as a "tour of God's world conducted by a minister of God with a cross and a round collar to prove it." He declares that he is collecting evidence to support his own concept of the Divinity:

13. See Dante *The Inferno.* I have used the Penguin Edition, translated by Dorothy L. Sayers (London: Penguin Books, 1949).

It's going to storm tonight—a terrific electric storm. Then you will see the Reverend T. Lawrence Shannon's conception of God Almighty paying a visit to the world he created. I want to go back to the Church and preach the gospel of God as Lightning and Thunder. . . and also stray dogs vivisected and . . . and . . . and . . . [*He points out suddenly toward the sea.*] That's him! There he is now! [*He is pointing out at a blaze, a majestic apocalypse of gold light, shafting the sky as the sun drops into the Pacific.*] (Act II, p. 57)

It is Hannah Jelkes who helps him up the way. For it is Hannah who suggests that he throw away violence and embrace the quiet virtue of compassion. There are, thereafter, two progressions: the movement of the old poet—an aging romantic—toward the completion of his life's work and the tortuous progress of Shannon toward forgiveness. Each of these "rebirths" is nursed by the woman whom the playwright describes (Act I, p. 18) as having the aspect of a "medieval saint."

Hannah Jelkes is one of Williams' few "good beings." She has the sensitivity of Alma or Blanche, but she undergirds her sympathy with moral strength. She has the beauty of the young girl Heavenly and she possesses, for Shannon, a marked sensuous appeal. But she has the will to resist his attempt to corrupt her through sexuality. Moreover, she not only has pity for him, she has the will to help him. She is able to accept his suffering and, when possible, to take steps to provide him with relief from pain. Most of all, Hannah Jelkes offers Shannon the gift of compassion, that human understanding which he has sought all of his life. As he lies writhing in the hammock, she looks within him and speaks of his obsessive sense of guilt:

Who wouldn't like to suffer and atone for the sins of himself and the world if it could be done in a hammock with ropes instead of nails, on a hill that's so much lovelier than Golgotha, the Place of the Skull, Mr. Shannon? There's something almost voluptuous in the way that you twist and groan in that hammock—no nails, no blood, no death. Isn't that a comparatively comfortable, almost voluptuous kind of crucifixion to suffer for the guilt of the world, Mr. Shannon? (Act III, p. 96)

Hannah, who mends "broken gates" between human beings, demonstrates Williams' transcendent morality. She reaches out to Shannon in compassion. She saves him in the same way she has saved her grandfather: through understanding. The poem, which synthesizes both lines of action, is completed almost at the moment when Shannon frees the captive iguana—and himself—from death:

> I cut loose one of God's creatures at the end of a rope.
>
> . . . .
>
> So that one of God's creatures could scramble home safe and free. . . .
> A little act of grace, Maxine. (Act III, p. 125)

A study of the whole range of Williams' drama shows the gradual development of a comprehensive moral structure. If his early works are concerned primarily with ethical implications within art—with the need for the integrity of self-expression—this playwright's later works have been increasingly concerned with the exploration of moral problems which are more comprehensive in nature. Williams' development as a moralist seems to have experienced three main phases of growth. His early plays are concerned with the struggle of the individual for self-realization. In the middle period of his development the playwright begins to equate his accounts of individual crisis with more universal phenomena, especially to trace their effect on society at large. In his later works Williams seems to relate these personal crises to the timeless progress of mankind in the moral universe.

It is significant to note that Williams' later works have taken on more and more of the apparatus of the orthodox Christian search for God. Gradually Williams' anti-hero—his symbol for modern man—has begun to assume the visage of the "negative saint," the great sinner, toiling up the steep ascent to God. Williams, whose admiration for Dante is demonstrated throughout his work, has thus followed the great poet in his definition of the moral function in art. Dante's position represents the Christian modification of the Aristotelian imperative to virtue. For the great Renaissance artist saw the theatre as an instrument designed to assist man toward a suprahuman mode of salvation. Williams, with his twentieth-century accounting of human transgression, attempts to serve much the same moral function as Dante: to articulate, transform, and purge human ills. His own words seem an appropriate conclusion to this discussion:

> [I]f there is any truth in the Aristotelian idea that violence is purged by its poetic representation on a stage, then it may be that my cycle of violent plays have had a moral justification after all. I know that I have felt it. I have always felt a release from the sense of meaninglessness and death when a work of tragic intention has seemed to me to have achieved that intention, even if only approximately, nearly.
>
> I would say that there is something much bigger in life and death than we have become aware of (or adequately recorded) in our living and dying. And, further, to compound this shameless romanticism, I would say that our serious theatre is a search for that something that is not yet successful but is still going on.
>
> (Preface, *Sweet Bird of Youth,* p. xi)

THE INCOMPLETE FABRIC

The drama of the American playwright Tennessee Williams represents a significant level of achievement in the total movement of Western theatre toward a distinctively contemporary form. There has developed around this playwright a highly articulate dramaturgy. A whole art of writing, staging, acting, and design has resulted which has synthesized elements drawn from European drama with purely native forms. Williams' form retains characteristic aspects of American cinema, dance, painting, and sculpture, as well as features drawn from the tradition of American poetry and fiction. Williams describes his theatric form as "plastic," as a kind of drama in which he has rewoven the complete fabric of the performing arts. Despite its debt to the theories and practices of earlier epochs, the theatre of Williams may be described as the image of a "new sensibility"; that is, its idea of form represents a major adjustment in the concept of dramatic imitation. Like other contemporary playwrights, Williams has transposed into the fabric of his drama a new perception of reality. The image of experience which appears in works such as *A Streetcar Named Desire* is not, however, entirely the creation of the dramatist. On the contrary, it is a symbol that owes its existence, in part, to the cultural history of the late nineteenth and twentieth centuries, especially to those explorations in thought which are given explication in the work of Hegel, Nietzsche, Darwin, Jung, Freud, Bergson, and others. Williams, like these thinkers, seeks to engage modern man in a search for new dimensions of truth, to develop within our time a "will-to-meaning."

Like other contemporary dramatists, Williams has attempted to restore to the theatre not only its creative power but also its moral function and its ritual power of carthársis. His drama takes the shape of a search for meaning which involves man at every level of his conscious experience. The form which the playwright has developed is in many senses synthetic. It represents an attempt to reconcile experience: to re-unify subjective, objective, and transcendental apprehensions of reality within the aesthetic form. But more than this, Williams attempts to create new realities, that is, to fashion images more coherent and more meaningful than the life which they represent. The poetry of his theatre may be described as a synthetic kind; it is composed in part from the fragments of past perspectives. Williams' drama employs for its interpretation of our own time this "synthetic myth," an interpretative structure pieced together from the conscious past of Western man.

Thus far, the drama of Williams has not seemed to achieve complete organic unity. Plays such as *The Glass Menagerie, A Streetcar Named Desire, Summer and Smoke, Cat on a Hot Tin Roof,* and *Camino Real* retain a fundamental internal antagonism, an inner conflict between experience and meaning, poetry and logic, appearance and reality. Later plays, especially

Suddenly Last Summer and *The Night of the Iguana,* show some signs of healing this aesthetic division, of achieving a more complete reconciliation within the form. This growing unity may be traced in part to the development in recent works of a more coherent rationale. If the plays produced between 1945 and 1955 are inclined toward moral skepticism and consequently to a limited internal development, the plays of the subsequent period—*Orpheus Descending, Suddenly Last Summer, Sweet Bird of Youth, Period of Adjustment,* and *The Night of the Iguana*—seem to reflect an increasingly sure moral position. In these later works, Williams comes to define the condition of man in terms very much like those of orthodox Christianity and to pose, therefore, for human redemption and reconciliation, the forgiveness of God. This "Christian" cycle of sin-suffering-expiation-redemption is perhaps most clearly defined in *The Night of the Iguana,* a play in which the protagonist seems to pass through all the stages of this progression in his time of life on the stage.

It is because of Williams' keen perception of the range of possibilities governing the inner life of modern man that his drama has proved so challenging to artists and to spectators throughout world theatre. Moreover, he demonstrates in his writing a rare gift for translating significant ideas into the popular language of the theatre. Although history must make the final judgment on his lasting achievement, it would now appear that Williams has made a major contribution both to the American theatre and to the development of a contemporary form of world drama; for he has exposed a large popular audience to much of the conventional intellectual apparatus through which the life of twentieth-century man is interpreted. His image of man and his concept of human crisis, his mythic apprehension of human transgression, and his plastic language have already become a permanent part of the theatrical syntax of world theatre.

The rise of Williams in the theatre of the twentieth century is not an accidental phenomenon. This dramatist, with his poetic penetration of the life of modern man, has made a distinctive contribution to the progress of the theatre toward a mature contemporary form.

appendix

PUBLISHED WORKS

Poetry

Five Young American Poets (Norfolk, Conn.: New Directions, 1944).
In the Winter of Cities (Norfolk, Conn.: New Directions, 1956).
See also *New Directions* Series XI, XII, XIII, and XIV.

Prose

One Arm and Other Stories (Norfolk, Conn.: New Directions, 1948).
The Roman Spring of Mrs. Stone (New York: New Directions, 1950).
Hard Candy: A Book of Stories (New York: New Directions, 1954).

Collections of Plays

27 Wagons Full of Cotton (Norfolk, Conn.: New Directions, 1946).
American Blues (New York: Dramatists Play Service, 1948).
Four Plays (*The Glass Menagerie, A Streetcar Named Desire, Summer and Smoke,* and *Camino Real*) (London: Secker and Warburg, 1956).

Three Players of a Summer Game (London: Secker and Warburg, 1960).
Garden District (London: Secker and Warburg, 1962).

Plays

Battle of Angels (limited ed.; New York: New Directions, 1945) (Pharos No. 1 and No. 2, Murray, Utah, distributors).
The Glass Menagerie (New York: Random House, 1945).
A Streetcar Named Desire (New York: New Directions, 1947).
Summer and Smoke (New York: New Directions, 1948).
The Rose Tattoo (New York: New Directions, 1951).
Camino Real (Norfolk, Conn.: New Directions, 1953).
Cat on a Hot Tin Roof (New York: New Directions, 1955).
Orpheus Descending (with *Battle of Angels*) (New York: New Directions, 1958).
Suddenly Last Summer (New York: New Directions, 1958) (Played, with *Something Unspoken,* as *Garden District,* New York, 1958).
Sweet Bird of Youth (New York: New Directions, 1959).
Period of Adjustment (New York: New Directions, 1960).
The Night of the Iguana (New York: New Directions, 1962).
The Milk Train Doesn't Stop Here Anymore (Norfolk, Conn.: New Directions, 1964).

Other Works

I Rise in Flame, Cried the Phoenix (limited ed.; Norfolk, Conn.: J. Laughlin, 1951) (A play about D. H. Lawrence with a note by Frieda Lawrence).
You Touched Me (with Donald Windham) (Boston: W. H. Baker, 1946).
Baby Doll (a film play) (New York: New Directions, 1956).
Lord Byron's Love Letters (New York: Ricordi, 1955) (A libretto for a one-act opera; taken from a short play of the same name and published in London, 1962).

OPENINGS

Battle of Angels, Wilbur Theatre, Boston, December 30, 1940; closed January 11, 1941.
The Glass Menagerie, Civic Theatre, Chicago, December 26, 1944; Playhouse Theatre, New York, March 31, 1945.
You Touched Me, Booth Theatre, New York, September 26, 1945.
A Streetcar Named Desire, Barrymore Theatre, New York, December 3, 1947.
Summer and Smoke, Music Box Theatre, New York, October 6, 1948.
The Rose Tattoo, Erlanger Theatre, Chicago, December 29, 1950; Martin Beck Theatre, New York, February 3, 1951.
Camino Real, Martin Beck Theatre, New York, March 19, 1953.
Cat on a Hot Tin Roof, Morosco Theatre, New York, March 24, 1955.
Orpheus Descending, Martin Beck Theatre, New York, March 21, 1957.
Garden District, York Theatre, New York, January 7, 1958.
Sweet Bird of Youth, Martin Beck Theatre, New York, March 10, 1959.
Period of Adjustment, The Helen Hays Theatre, New York, November 10, 1960.
The Night of the Iguana, Royale Theatre, New York, December 28, 1961.
The Milk Train Doesn't Stop Here Anymore, Morosco Theatre, New York, January 10, 1963.

PERMISSIONS GRANTED IN FOREIGN COUNTRIES

The Glass Menagerie

Argentina
Australia
Austria
Belgium
Canada
Ceylon
Chile
Czechoslovakia
Denmark
Finland
Germany
Great Britain
Holland
Hong Kong
Hungary
Iceland
India
Ireland
Israel
Italy
Japan
Malaya
Mexico
New Zealand
Norway
Pakistan
The Philippines
Poland
Portugal
Rumania
South Africa
Southern Rhodesia
Spain
Sweden
Switzerland
Uruguay

A Streetcar Named Desire

Argentina
Australia
Austria
Belgium
Canada
Chile
Cyprus
Czechoslovakia
Denmark
Egypt
Finland
France
Germany
Great Britain
Greece
Holland
Hungary
Iceland
Israel
Italy
Japan
Korea
Mexico
Morocco
New Zealand
Norway
Poland
Portugal
South Africa
Spain
Sudan
Sweden
Switzerland
Turkey
Uruguay
Yugoslavia

Cat on a Hot Tin Roof

Argentina
Australia
Austria
Belgium
Canada
Chile
Cyprus
Denmark
Egypt
Finland
France
Germany
Greece
Holland
Iceland
Israel
Italy
Japan
Mexico
New Zealand
Norway
Portugal
South Africa
Sweden
Switzerland
Turkey
Uruguay
Yugoslavia

selected bibliography

Albérès, René-Marill (pseud.). See Marill, René.

Apollonio, Umbro. "Expressionism," in *Encyclopedia of World Art,* V. New York: McGraw Hill, 1961. Pp. 311–23.

Appia, Adolphe. "The Future of Production," in *Theatre Arts Anthology,* eds. Rosamond Gilder *et al.* New York: Theatre Arts Books, 1950. Pp. 519–33.

Aristotle. *Ethics,* trans. D. P. Chase. London: J. M. Dent and Sons, 1911.

Artaud, Antonin. *The Theater and Its Double,* trans. Mary Caroline Richards. New York: Grove Press, 1958.

Auerbach, Erich. *Mimesis: The Representation of Reality in Western Literature,* trans. Willard R. Trask. Princeton: Princeton University Press, 1953.

Bentley, Eric. *In Search of Theater.* New York: Alfred Knopf, 1953.

Bergson, Henri. *An Introduction to Metaphysics,* trans. T. E. Hulme. New York: The Liberal Arts Press, 1949.

Bergson, Henri. *Laughter,* trans. Cloudesley Brereton and Fred Rothwell. New York: The Macmillan Company, 1911.

Bochumer Diskussion über "Camino Real" von Tennessee Williams. (Transcription of the Bochum Festival.) Frankfurt-am-Main: S. Fischer Verlag, 1955. Pp. 5–14.

Browne, E. Martin. Preface to *Cat on a Hot Tin Roof.* London: Penguin Books, 1956.

Butcher, S. H., trans. *Aristotle's Theory of Poetry and Fine Art: With a Critical Text and Translation of* The Poetics (4th ed. rev.). New York: Dover Publications, 1951.

Carter, Huntly. *The New Spirit in the European Theatre.* London: Ernest Benn, Ltd., 1925.

Clark, Barrett. *European Theories of the Drama* (rev. ed.). New York: Crown Publishers, 1947.

Cocteau, Jean. *La Machine Infernale.* Paris: Editions Bernard Grasset, 1934.

Coleridge, Samuel Taylor. *Coleridge's Shakespearean Criticism,* ed. Thomas Middleton Raysor. 2 vols. Cambridge: Harvard University Press, 1936.

The Complete Greek Drama, eds. Whitney J. Oates and Eugene O'Neill, Jr. 2 vols. New York: Random House, 1938.

Eisenstein, Sergei. *The Film Sense,* trans. Jay Leyda. New York: Harcourt, Brace, and Company, 1947.

Esslin, Martin. *Bertolt Brecht: A Choice of Evils.* London: Eyre and Spottiswoode, 1959.

Falk, Doris V. *Eugene O'Neill and The Tragic Tension.* New Brunswick, New Jersey: Rutgers University Press, 1958.

Fergusson, Francis. *Dante's Drama of the Mind.* Princeton: Princeton University Press, 1953.

———. *The Idea of a Theater.* Princeton: Princeton University Press, 1949.

Gassner, John. *Masters of the Drama* (3d ed. rev.). New York: Dover Publications, 1954.

Hamilton, Edith. *The Greek Way to Western Civilization.* ("Mentor Books.") New York: New American Library, 1948.

Hegel, Georg W. F. *Lectures on Aesthetics,* in *The Philosophy of Hegel,* ed. Carl J. Friedrich; trans. Bernard Bosanquet and William M. Bryant. New York: Modern Library, No. 239, 1953, 1954. Pp. 333–95.

Hering, Doris. "Valerie Bettis Choreographs Streetcar Named Desire," *Dance,* XXVI (December, 1952), 20–21, 59.

Horace. *The Art of Poetry,* trans. H. Rushton Fairclough in *Horace.* London: William Heinemann, 1926. Pp. 442–89.

Howard, Leon. *Literature and the American Tradition.* Garden City, New York: Doubleday and Company, 1960.

Jackson, Esther M. "The Problem of Form in the Drama of Tennessee Williams," *College Language Association Journal,* IV, No. 1 (September, 1960), 8–21.

———. "Music and Dance as Elements of Form in the Drama of Tennessee Williams," *Revue d'Histoire du Théâtre,* XV, No. 3 (1963), 294–301.

———. "The Emergence of the Anti-hero in the Contemporary Drama," *The Central States Speech Journal,* XII, No. 2 (1960–61), 92–99.

Jaspers, Karl. *Reason and Existenz: Five Lectures,* trans. William Earle. New York: Noonday Press, 1955.

Jung, Carl Gustav. *Collected Works,* eds. Herbert Read, Michael Fordham, and Gerhard Adler, trans. R. F. C. Hull. ("Bollingen Series XX.") 17 vols. (in process). London: Routledge and Kegan Paul, and New York: Pantheon Books, 1953–6?.

"Concerning the Archetypes, With Special Reference to the Anima Concept," in *The Archetypes and the Collective Unconscious,* vol. IX, Part I (1959).

Freud and Psychoanalysis, vol. IV (1961).

"Psychology of Transference," in *The Practice of Psychotherapy,* vol. XVI (1954).

———. *Modern Man in Search of a Soul,* trans. W. S. Dell and C. F. Baynes. New York: Harcourt, Brace, and Company, 1934.

———. *Psychological Types,* trans. H. Godwin Baynes. London: Routledge and Kegan Paul, 1923.

Kandinsky, Wassily. *Concerning the Spiritual in Art,* trans. Francis Golffing *et al.* New York: Wittenborn and Schultz, Inc., 1947.

Kant, Immanuel. *Critique of Aesthetic Judgment,* trans. James Creed Meredith. Oxford: The Clarendon Press, 1911.

———. *Critique of Aesthetical Judgement,* trans. J. H. Bernard in *Kant: Selections,* ed. Theodore Meyer Greene. ("Modern Student's Library," Philosophy Series.) New York: Charles Scribner's Sons, 1929. Pp. 375–444.

Kazan, Elia. "Notebook for *A Streetcar Named Desire*" in *Directing the Play,* eds. Toby Cole and Helen Krich Chinoy. Indianapolis: Bobbs Merrill Company, 1953. Pp. 296–310.

Kitto, H. D. F. *Greek Tragedy: A Literary Study* (rev. ed.). ("Doubleday Anchor Books," A38.) Garden City, New York: Doubleday and Company, 1954.

Klee, Paul. *The Inward Vision: Watercolors, Drawings, Writings,* trans. Norbert Guterman. New York: Harry N. Abrams, 1958.

Langer, Susanne K. *Problems of Art: Ten Philosophical Lectures.* New York: Charles Scribner's Sons, 1957.

Lawrence, D. H. *Studies in Classic American Literature.* New York: T. Seltzer, 1923.

Lawson, Joan. "Ballet Theatre in London," *Dancing Times,* LXVII (October, 1956), 17–19.

Lawson, John Howard. *Theory and Technique of Playwriting.* New York: G. P. Putnam's Sons, 1936.

Macgowan, Kenneth. *The Theatre of Tomorrow.* New York: Boni and Liveright, 1921.

Marill, René. *La Révolte des écrivains d'aujourd'hui.* Paris: Correa, 1949.

Miller, Arthur. *Collected Plays.* New York: The Viking Press, 1957.

———. "On Social Plays" in the Preface to *A View from the Bridge.* London: The Cresset Press, 1960. Pp. 7–24.

Myers, Bernard S. *The German Expressionists.* New York: Frederick A. Praeger, 1957.

Nietzsche, Friedrich. *The Birth of Tragedy* and *The Genealogy of Morals,* trans. Francis Golffing. ("Doubleday Anchor Books," A81.) Garden City, New York: Doubleday and Company, 1956.

O'Neill, Eugene. *The Iceman Cometh.* New York: Random House, 1946.

Pirandello, Luigi. *Six Characters in Search of an Author,* in *Naked Masks: Five Plays,* ed. Eric Bentley, trans. Edward Storer. ("Everyman's Library," No. 47A.) New York: E. P. Dutton, 1952.

Progoff, Ira. *Jung's Psychology and Its Social Meaning.* New York: Julian Press, 1953.

Read, Herbert. *A Concise History of Modern Painting.* New York: Frederick A. Praeger, 1959.

———. *The Philosophy of Modern Art.* New York: Horizon Press, 1952.

Saintsbury, George. *A History of Criticism.* 3 vols. Edinburgh: William Blackwood and Sons, 1900–1904.

Sartre, Jean-Paul. "Forgers of Myth," *Theatre Arts,* XXX (June, 1946), 324–35.

———. *No Exit and Three Other Plays,* trans. Stuart Gilbert. New York: Vintage Books, 1955.

Schlemmer, Oskar, *et al. The Theatre of the Bauhaus,* trans. Arthur S. Wensinger. Middletown, Connecticut: Wesleyan University Press, 1961.

Schopenhauer, Arthur. *The World as Will and Idea,* trans. R. B. Haldane and J. Kemp. 3 vols. London: Kegan Paul, 1896.

Shank, Theodore. "Provincialism in College and University Play Selec-

tion, A Five-Year Study," *The Educational Theatre Journal,* XIII (May, 1961), 112–17.
Sievers, W. David. *Freud on Broadway*. New York: Hermitage House, 1955.
Stahl, Norma G. "Converting Literature into Dance," *Dance,* XXVII (March, 1953), 16–18, 47–48.
Stambusky, Alan A. "Significant College and University Play Production Patterns in 1961–62," *The Educational Theatre Journal,* XV (May, 1963), 163–65.
Strindberg, August. *Six Plays of Strindberg,* trans. Elizabeth Sprigge. ("Doubleday Anchor Book," A54.) Garden City, New York: Doubleday and Company, 1955.
Van Doren, Mark, ed. Introduction to *Hamlet* in *Four Great Tragedies*. New York: Pocket Books, Inc., 1955. Pp. 201–12; originally published in *Shakespeare*. New York: Henry Holt and Company, 1939.
Wagner, Richard. *Opera and Drama,* trans. Edwin Evans. 2 vols. London: William Reeves, 1913.
Weitz, Morris. "The Role of Theory in Aesthetics," *The Journal of Aesthetics,* XV (September, 1956), 27–35.
Williams, Tennessee. See the Appendix.

index